250

BLESSED
EVEREST

BLESSED
EVEREST

Climb to the summit of Mount Everest with BRIAN BLESSED,
Britain's own actor/adventurer

BRIAN BLESSED

a Salamander book

Published by Salamander Books Limited
LONDON

A Salamander Book

I dedicate this book to Alison Hargreaves, a great climber and an inspiration to all lovers of adventure.

Published by Salamander Books Ltd
129-137 York Way
London N7 9LG
United Kingdom

© Salamander Books Ltd, 1995

Text © Brian Blessed, 1995

ISBN 0 86101 828 1

All correspondence concerning the content of this volume should be addressed to Salamander Books Ltd.

CREDITS
Commissioning Editor: Tony Hall
Designer: John Heritage
Map and colour artwork: Janos Marffy (© Salamander Books Ltd)
Filmset: SX Composing Ltd, England
Colour reproduction: P&W Graphics Pte Ltd, Singapore

9 8 7 6 5 4 3 2 1

Printed in Italy

Page 1: *A Tibetan bronze of a form of the Buddhist deity Avalokitesvara, the Merciful Lord. The deity is the manifestation of the eternal Buddha and is reincarnated in each successive Dalai Lama.*
Pages 2-3: *The camera used by Dr Alexander Kellas during the reconnaissance expedition of 1921. Dr Kellas died at Kampa Dzong. Everest from the due west, seen from the peak of Gokyo Ri, at 18,000 feet (5,400 m).*
Page 5: *An ice axe from an Everest expedition of the 1920s.*
Page 6: *A Tibetan thangka, or painted wall hanging, depicting the birth of Sagarmatha – Mount Everest.*
Page 7: *Brian Blessed in the Western Cwm, with the Southwest Cwm behind, during his climb in 1993.*

CONTENTS

To all lovers of adventure,

I cordially invite you to join me, Brian Blessed, on a thrilling, epic expedition to the very roof of the world, the mighty Himalayas.

On our adventure we will pass through ancient lands and encounter rare animals and fascinating people with strange customs.

Finally, following the footsteps of our heroes, and facing the same dangers they encountered, we will arrive at the foot of Mount Everest itself, and slowly, step by step, ascend its gigantic ridges to the summit of the highest mountain in the world.

So stop whatever you are doing and join me on this wonderful voyage of discovery.

Good Luck and Best Wishes,

Brian Blessed

BRIAN BLESSED

'in the evening light this country can be beautiful . . . shadows soften the hillsides; there is a blending of lines and folds . . . so that one comes to bless the absolute bareness, feeling that here is a pure beauty of form, a kind of ultimate harmony'.
GEORGE LEIGH MALLORY, 1921[1]

THE BIRTH OF MOUNT EVEREST

THERE IS A LEGEND about how the world's greatest mountain range – the Himalayas – was formed.

In the beginning, according to an ancient Indian work, *The Mababharata*, the god of Vishnu, The Preserver of Life, lived on the northern shore of a great sea. His only companions were a pair of seagulls. Each year the female gull laid her eggs close to the shore but each year the sea washed the eggs away. The female gull tried building her nest further inland but to no avail: every year the sea advanced further and further over the land, seeking out and destroying her eggs. Eventually the gulls cried out in anguish to Vishnu to help them. Vishnu opened his mouth and swallowed the sea, which vanished as though it had never been and in its place lay the newly created Mother Earth.

As Vishnu slept, exhausted after a bout of drinking, the Demon Hiranyanksha leapt onto Mother Earth and ravaged her with such terrible violence, that her limbs were broken and levered up high into the clouds, thus forming the Himalayas.

Geology tells us a rather different story. It says that, about 50 million years ago, there was a large sea, called Tethys, that gently lapped the shores of Asia – what is now Tibet. This idyllic land was clothed in magnificent forests, filled with a great variety of wildlife. The dragonfly *Epiophlebia Laidlawii* (the Living Fossil), which inhabited these forests, still exists to this day. However, the tranquil landscape was to change dramatically. Over many centuries, a vast continent known as Gondwanaland moved slowly across Tethys and collided with this

Above: *A 16th century Tibetan bronze inlayed with silver and gold, portraying the figure of a deified lama.*

Left: *A view of the Himalayas from space, looking north. From here they do indeed look like 'a ring of white fire'.*

Right: *Mount Everest from space, with the early morning light striking the surrounding peaks. The mountain itself is just left of centre. The white face in the centre is the Kangshung Face. Tibet is to the north.*

ancient shore, forcing the soft sedimentary rock of Asia dramatically upwards, as the harder granites, basalts, and gneisses of Gondwanaland bit into it. This squeezing, wrenching and twisting resulted in the creation of the highest, yet youngest, of the mountain ranges – the Himalayas.

The name 'Himalayas' means 'abode of snow'. It stretches, without interruption, across the top of India in a gentle curve for 1,500 miles (2,400 m) between the Brahmaputra and Indus rivers. And the core of this colossal squeeze is Mount Everest!

The Geology of Everest

Everest is an enormous pyramid with three great ridges and three wide faces. The lower level of the mountain is composed mainly of metamorphic rocks, which came up from the Earth's mantle. They are called schists and are coarse-grained and crystalline. Among the schists are gneisses and migmatites, which were created under profound heat and stress. Higher up, we find a huge amount of granite and above this are sedimentary rocks, which were laid down under the Tethys Sea. The clays, silts and chalky remains of marine animals were transformed into shale, pelites, sandstone and limestone.

Everest climbers affectionately know them as the 'yellow band', which is on Everest's South Face. The summit pyramid of the great mountain is made up of a purer limestone with sandy layers. It is astonishing, but the highest peak of the world was formed 325 million years ago on the bed of an ancient sea, which is now extinct.

The Blank Space on the Map

It is hard to envisage the vast scale of the Himalayas. Such is the size of this mountain range, that if we imagine the most westerly point to be London, then the most easterly would be somewhere near Moscow.

The mountain land of the Himalayas that bounds India on the north like a huge wall of rock, is often called 'the backbone of the world'. Great rivers carve immense gorges throughout this amazing landscape. It is divided roughly into three zones.

Rising from the Indian plains are the foothills of the forested Siwaliks, a natural habitat for creatures like the cobra, bear, tiger and the amazing lunar moth, 'Edwards' Atlas', which has a wing-span of 10 inches (25 cm) or more. Beyond the Siwaliks, rise the strangely named 'Lesser Himalayas'. This name always brings a smile to my face, for the region of the Lesser Himalayas contains hundreds of peaks that are 15,000 feet (4,500 m) or more in height. However, they are 'lesser', when compared to the incredible 'Greater Himalayas', which is a land of

astonishing gigantic mountains. Ninety-one summits exceed 24,000 feet (7,200 m); all of them are higher than any other mountain in the rest of the world. Thirteen super giants top 26,000 feet (7,800 m). But towering above them all in total supremacy at 29,028 feet – 5½ miles (8.8 km) high – is Mount Everest.

Experts claim that it is only 'a youngster' and still has a lot of growing to do. They say that in 40 million years it will be 80,000 feet (24,000 m) in height. My friends, if this is the case, we had better hurry up and climb it before it gets any higher.

Nestled among the mountains towards the eastern end of the Himalayas is the magical kingdom of Nepal. To the north, is the equally fascinating country of Tibet. Mount Everest is partly in Nepal and partly in Tibet and the great mountain has been known to these two civilisations for centuries. The rest of the world was in total ignorance of its existence. The earliest record in the Western world is dated 1733. D'Anville of Paris published a map of Tibet, which correctly marked the position of the mountain and named it 'Tschoumou-Lancma'. The map was based on the work of a group of French Capuchin friars who, between 1707 and 1733, lived in Lhasa, the capital of Tibet. But it wasn't until 1852, in India, that the legend began. In that year, the Bengali Chief Computer, an Anglo-Indian named Hennessey, rushed into the office of Sir Andrew Waugh, the Surveyor General in Dehra-Dun, and exclaimed: "Sir! I have discovered the highest mountain in the world!"

It was known at the time as 'Peak XV'. Sir Andrew Waugh named the mountain 'Everest' after Sir George Everest, his predecessor, the Surveyor-General of India. Afterwards it was discovered that the mountain had many names, such as Kangchen Lemboo Geudyong, Devadhunga, Chingopamaqi, Jo-Mo-Glan-Ma and the Turquoise Mountain. The Chinese call it Qomolangma-Feng and the Great Headache Mountain. The Nepalese have recently named it Sagarmatha and the Tibetans call it Chomolungma, which means 'Goddess Mother of the World'. But the name that Sir Andrew Waugh gave it in 1852 is still the one by which it is most known.

Exploring the Himalayas

You must understand that at this time in history Tibet was a forbidden country. It was ruled by a legendary 'god king' – the Dalai Lama – who resided in his vast palace 'The Potala', in Lhasa. On entering this kingdom, the surveyors, if captured, faced torture and death. Yet this did not stop them and, using all manner of disguises, they succeeded in mapping out huge areas of unknown land.

But the dream and goal of explorers and mountaineers to reach and possibly climb Everest seemed impossible. The Himalayan passes that led to the mountain were walled, barricaded and guarded by hostile Tibetan soldiers. It was the same story from Nepal. The King there also closed his country to all foreigners.

Then a miracle happened. In 1913, a handsome captain, called John Baptist Lucius Noel, serving with the British Army in Northern India, resolved to get past the Tibetan border guards and head for Everest. He pretended to be a half-caste Indian and dyed his hair black and skin brown. His disguise was perfect. Accompanied by five Nepalese Sherpas and carrying their own food and tents, they set off on their epic journey to the Tibetan border. After many weeks of hardship they found the high mountain pass, Chorten Nyima La (19,000 feet – 5,700 m) that the Tibetans didn't watch and powered on to Everest.

On the dry Tibetan plain, they experienced the fierce west wind that filled their noses and throats with dry dust and made breathing very difficult. The fierce sun penetrated the thin air and scorched their skins, and at night the temperatures plummeted way below zero.

Despite all this, they at last caught sight of Everest, only 40 miles (64 km) away, towering head and shoul-

ders above a high mountain range. It was a fine achievement and was the closest a Westerner had ever come to the mountain.

Captain Noel was eager to press on, for it was rumoured that high on Everest there was a mysterious place in the snows called the Rongbuk Monastery, which housed many nuns and monks and was ruled over by a holy Lama, who was the incarnation of a god called Chongraysay.

But he could not reach it. It was heartbreaking, having got so far, to be stopped by Tibetan soldiers and peremptorily ordered to leave the country. They were lucky to escape with their lives.

At a meeting of the Royal Geographical Society in March 1919, Captain Noel delivered a lecture about his journey into Tibet. He said, "Now that the North and South Poles have been reached, we must turn our eyes to the third pole – Everest."

Everest was often referred to as 'The Third Pole'. Captain Noel's lecture aroused great enthusiasm and the president of the Alpine Club, Captain Percy Farrar, spoke of climbing to Everest's summit itself. This, said Sir Frances Younghusband, was the decisive leap forward. Younghusband asked Sir Charles Bell, the political officer for Tibetan affairs, to visit the Dalai Lama in

Left: *The members of the 1921 Reconnaissance expedition which explored the northern approaches to the mountain through Tibet, and found a way through the East Rongbuk Glacier to the North Col. From the left, back row: Wollaston, Howard-Bury (leader), Heron, Raeburn (climbing leader). Seated: Leigh Mallory, Wheeler, Bullock, Morshead. The expedition's oxygen expert Dr. Kellas died before the mountain was reached.*

Lhasa and ask for permission to climb Everest. Bell and the Dalai Lama had been good friends for many years. Bell succeeded. And so, at last permission was granted for a British expedition.

It was a momentous occasion and there was much rejoicing! The news that the expedition was definitely to take place was given at a meeting of the Royal Geographical Society, in London, on 10 January 1921. The excitement of it all thrilled everyone! The newspapers had a field day with headlines like "Where White Man Has Never Trod" and "Miles Higher Than Man Has Ever Been".

The First Expedition

In the spring of 1921 the exploring expedition, also called the 'Reconnaissance', set off.

Colonel Howard Bury, a gentleman who lived in Ireland, was the leader. Mr Raeburn, a veteran Alpine climber, Dr Kellas, Mr Mallory and Mr Bullock formed the mountaineering party. Major Morshead, Captain Wheeler and Dr Heron were the surveyors and Dr Wollaston was the naturalist and medical officer. Interpreter, porters and native cooks, recruited in India, completed the expedition's personnel.

In 1921, the Reconnaissance expedition had to make a sweep across the plains of Tibet through unknown country. Hopes ran high and news of discoveries was eagerly awaited at home. But experts were unsure: "They will have problems enough just finding the mountain, without attempting to do anything else!"

People laughed at this; but it was true. There were many obstacles to overcome, giant mountain ranges to traverse, deep gorges and raging rivers to cross. It took them a long time to unravel the geography of the deserts of Tibet and the bewildering valleys that led up to Everest's northern glaciers.

At a fort called Khampa Dzong, a great misfortune befell them. Dr Kellas, who had been ill for many days, died of dysentery. This was a terrible blow but still they pressed on.

As the expedition moved closer to Everest, they knew that they were 'stepping off the map'.

From this group of brave explorers emerged a man in the truly heroic mould, who was to be the first, and possibly the greatest, challenger Everest ever knew, George Leigh Mallory. His name was to become synonymous with that great mountain. He was nicknamed 'Sir Galahad' after that famous knight, and became a legend in his own lifetime. Tall, handsome, and a fine mountaineer, it was his task to find a possible route up the mountain.

Finally, the party reached the Rongbuk Valley, the main approach to Everest, and before their eyes lay the Rongbuk Monastery! It wasn't a fairy tale after all! It actually existed – the highest monastery in the world, standing at 16,400 feet (4,920 m). There to greet them were hundreds of nuns and monks and the holy Lama himself, the reincarnation of the god Chongraysay.

Higher up the valley, Mallory said, the Rongbuk glacier surged upwards, like 'the charge of the Light Brigade', for 16 miles (25 km) to the base of the mountain. They had arrived! Mallory described the moment:

> Rising from the bright mists, Everest above was imminent, vast, forceful, no fleeting apparition of elusive dream form; nothing could have been more set and permanent – more terrific – more unconquerable.

How this mountain obsessed him! He threw his whole body and soul into the fight against it.

The monks at the monastery greeted the expedition with the words "Tashidelhi", which means "How do you do?". They then told the explorers of fearful beings who inhabited the snows around Everest, called 'Nitikanji', or 'Snow Men'. They also had other names like 'Sukpa' or 'Yeti'. The monks said that they were known to kill men, carry off women, and to bite the necks of Yaks, the Tibetan ox, and drink their blood. "What are they?" enquired the explorers. "Man, ape, bear?" They received no satisfactory answer. The

Below: *In the Tibetan fortress of Shekar Dzong the 'White Glass Fort' sits the Dzong Pen – or lord – who greeted Mallory and the first Everest expedition with sweetmeats and Tibetan tea. The remains of this remarkable fortress can be seen on page 99. Behind the Dzong Pen are examples of the Tibetan religious wall hangings or thangka.*

SIR HUNT:
- Les sherpas
ont vu
L'HOMME
DES NEIGES
VOIR SUITE PAGE 2

Left: *One of the great mysteries of the Himalayas is the existence of the Yeti, or Abominable Snowman. Though no one has ever seen the creature, it still grips the popular imagination, and expeditions continue to be sent out into the wild mountains in an attempt to prove its existence.*

Below: *What physical evidence exists for the Yeti comes mostly from expeditions to Everest and her surrounding Himalayan peaks. This awe-inspiring (and not a little scary) footprint was photographed by Eric Shipton during the Cho-Oyu expedition of 1952. It measured over two feet (.6 m) long.*

Abominable Snowman, as it was later called, remained a mystery, as it is even today.

The monks also warned the climbers about demons and goblins called 'Yi-Dag' or 'Preta', that could appear without warning and cause a great deal of trouble, and demons like 'Srin-Po', who would eat the limbs of men,

or 'Srul-Po', a female demon, who caused illness in children. Then there was 'Snyo-Byed', who made people go mad and the dreaded 'Zhidag', who threw rocks!

The First Attempt

From early spring, through summer to late autumn, the bold explorers inspired by the indomitable spirit and energy of Mallory, attempted to scale the mighty mountain.

You must understand that they were dressed only in Norfolk jackets, plus-fours, puttees (army gaiters), homburg hats and simple windproofs. Thus inadequately clothed, they braved the savage moods of Everest. All these dangers they shared with the equally brave Sherpas.

Finally, on 24 September 1921, Mallory, Bullock and Wheeler, with three Sherpas, made the first attempt to reach the summit and managed to get up the North Col of the mountain to a height of 23,100 feet (6,930 m) – just 6,000 feet (1,800 m) short of the summit! A terrific achievement!

The surveyors also excelled and made an original survey of some 12,000 square miles (30,000 sq/km), plus a detailed photographic survey of the 600 miles (960 km) immediately surrounding Mount Everest. There was no doubt at all that the expedition was a great success.

The North Side Expeditions

In 1922, the British came back, this time with a much more powerful climbing team.

The expedition was commanded by the world renowned Himalayan explorer, General CG Bruce. "The very best man" was how everyone at that time described him. His brilliant leadership brought the expedition's caravan of 400 animals and 100 men safely over 350 miles (560 km) of difficult terrain from India to the foot of Mount Everest. He established headquarters or base camp at 17,000 feet (5,100 m), from where he organised the lines of communication on the East Rongbuk glacier, which was considered the best approach to the mountain.

After a distance of 16 miles (25 km) along the glacier at approximately 21,500 feet (6,450 m) you arrive at the base of the North Col, or Chang-La, as the Tibetans call it. A col, by the way, is a dip in a ridge often between two peaks. In this case the North Col at 23,100 feet (36,960 m) is between a mountain called Changse (North Peak) 24,780 feet (39,648 m) and Everest itself.

From the top of the North Col the route follows the North Ridge of Everest, which is largely composed of snow and rock, to 27,000 feet (43,200 m). From this point there is a traverse across the North Face to the

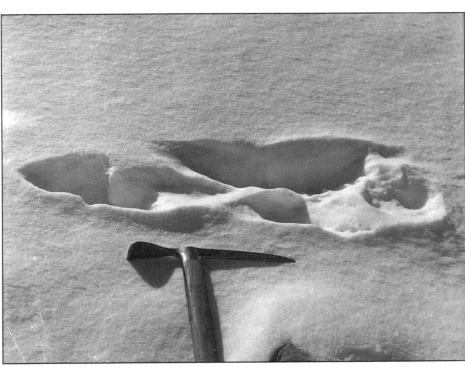

given Roman numerals, Camp I, II, III, and so on, until there was only 2,000 feet (600 m) between the highest camp and the summit. Oxygen, for the first time was introduced. The apparatus was designed by the Air Ministry and consisted of a Bergen pack frame holding four Swedish steel cylinders, tubes and regulator valves and a simple breathing mask or pipe mouthpiece of copper and chamois leather. A full bottle of oxygen weighed 5¾ lbs (2.3 kg), and the total weight of the apparatus with four bottles was 33 lbs (13 kg). Ten sets were made, four of them spares. Four cylinders would supply oxygen to a climber above the North Col for about seven hours.

The actual climbing team numbered eight. They were a varied bunch of characters, bearing such colourful names as Somerville, Norton, Wakefield, Strutt, Morshead, Mallory (once more), Longstaff and the Australian, George Finch. George Finch, by the way, was the father of Peter Finch, the famous film actor. All of them, except Finch, objected to using oxygen on Everest, maintaining that it was unsporting and therefore 'not British'. They felt that if the mountain *could* be climbed without oxygen, then it *should* be climbed without it. Mallory himself saw in oxygen a challenge to the human spirit of adventure and an attack by science upon natural values.

Altitude

Everyone agreed, of course, that breathing on Everest was a formidable difficulty. Allow me to explain a few facts about altitude. As a climber goes higher and higher the amount of oxygen in the air decreases because the air pressure steadily falls. It is interesting to note that if you stand on the summit of Mount Kilimanjaro, at 19,340 feet (5,802 m), the highest mountain in Africa, you will experience breathing air that is one half of its sea level pressure. On Everest's summit it is about one third. It is generally agreed that above 22,500 feet (6,750 m) on Everest, the human body deteriorates, which is why it is called 'the death zone'. From this height, the higher you go, the more rapid the deterioration. Don't worry, it's just as bad as it sounds!

Let's now look on the bright side. How does the human body adapt to this hostile environment? It was discovered that with increasing altitude there is an increase in the number and concentration of red blood cells (erythrocytes) that contain oxygen. Quite simply, this increase in red cells compensates for the lack of oxygen at altitude. The higher you get, the more red cells you produce. However, this process has to be given time. Breathing becomes deeper and faster, the heart rate is raised, the blood thickens considerably and there is a

Above: *Braving the might of Everest without oxygen and with only tweeds and sturdy leather boots for protection, Mallory and Norton approach 26,800 feet (8,040 m), during the expedition of 1922. It was to be the highest point climbed to date.*

shoulder of Everest, where it meets the North East Ridge. (Traverse means to climb horizontally across a feature.) Along this North East Ridge are the two rocky points called the First Step at 28,000 feet (8,400 m) and the Second Step at 28,250 feet (8,475 m). Above the last step is the Final Pyramid which leads to the summit.

The Polar Method

The attack on Everest was to be made by the 'polar method', first used in the Arctic and Antarctic regions. This method involved setting up a series of camps, approximately 2,000 feet (600 m) apart, each stocked with food and equipment. To identify them, they were

real danger of thrombosis and strokes. The speed of acclimatisation varies but the safest course is to gain height gradually and not stay at high altitude for too long. Most Everest climbers suffer acclimatisation symptoms, which include headaches, insomnia, nausea and, more rarely, pulmonary or cerebral oedema – i.e. fluid accumulating on the lungs (pulmonary) or on the brain (cerebral). Oedemas are extremely dangerous – a climber must retreat to lower altitudes for recovery, as the condition can be fatal.

Out of interest, science informs us that there is a large mass of very cold air in the stratosphere 30 miles (50 km) above the Equator. This cold air is very heavy and increases the pressure below at altitudes of about 2-9 miles (4-16 km) above the Earth's surface. The summits of the highest mountains, including Mount Everest, come within its range and this pressure forms what little thin air there is on the summit. In other words, this climatic idiosyncrasy makes it just possible to reach the highest point on Earth breathing natural air. We are dealing here with conditions at the limit of human tolerance. From this, you can see that if Mount Everest were situated at a higher latitude (for example, outside London) it would be impossible for a climber to reach the summit without supplementary oxygen, for the simple reason that the mountain would not possess any air at all near its summit, due to lack of atmospheric pressure at so northerly a point.

Back in 1922, knowledge of altitude was in its infancy. I have talked about the clothes they wore, and here's a little information about their footwear and equipment.

Equipment and Cost

Four kinds of footwear were recommended: ski boots; un-nailed felt boots with lambskin legs to the knee; high moccasins, ordered from Canada; and Finneskoes,

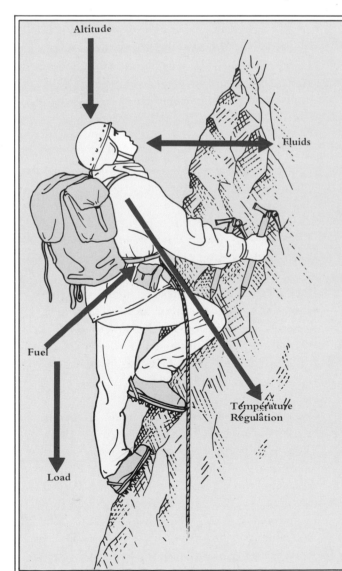

Altitude

Fluids

Fuel

Temperature Regulation

Load

SURVIVING AT ALTITUDE

Climbing above 22,500 (6,750 m) the human body begins to deteriorate. In fact due to lack of oxygen and low atmospheric pressure at these high altitudes, the body is actually dying. Without a constant awareness of the dangers of altitude, a climber's life will always be in danger. To guard against altitude sickness, expeditions are always organized around lengthy periods of acclimatisation.

Altitude As a climber ascends, the heartbeat quickens, and at the same time blood thickens. If a climber is not physiologically conditioned to these changes, serious health problems can result.

Fluids Dehydration is a real danger at altitude. Without realising it a climber can lose enormous amounts of fluid from his body through sweating and hard breathing in the cold dry air. It is absolutely vital that he drinks at least four litres of fluid per day.

Fuel Exertion at high altitude quickly saps the body of its strength. A high carbohydrate diet of 3,000–4,000 calories keeps the body supplied.

Load Weight of packs carried must be kept to a minimum, particularly on a summit attempt.

Temperature Regulation With temperatures capable of dropping to 25 degrees below zero, frostbite and sore throats are a constant problem. Strong ultra violet light at high altitude can also lead to snow blindness and sunburn.

ordered from Norway. All footwear was made to accommodate three pairs of rough socks. Crampons were made of light Duralumin. Ropes were made of hemp and sometimes silk. Though hemp was strong, it could freeze up and prove inflexible on the mountain.

The combined cost of the 1921 and 1922 expeditions came to about £8,000. Most of the money was provided by The Royal Geographical Society and The Alpine Club. Notable people who contributed were King George V, £100, the Prince of Wales, £50, and the Viceroy of India – Lord Reading, who gave 750 rupees.

A fine and varied amount of food was taken on the expedition such as chicken breasts, salmon, pastes, oxtail, mock turtle and cream of chicken soups, spanish olives, capers, horse-radish powder, Oxford marmalade and peppermint creams. Primus stoves were taken for cooking and, all in all, it was a well organised expedition that was in deadly earnest about getting to the top of Everest.

Once it had arrived at the mountain, the 1922 expedition performed splendidly. Captain Noel for instance, with his fine group of Sherpas, carried his 35 lb (14 kg) film camera to the top of the North Col. A world record! The heroic Mallory, Somerville and Norton reached 26,995 feet (8,098 m) without oxygen. Shortly after this epic climb, George Finch and Captain Geoffrey Bruce (a young cousin of the general) using the primitive oxygen apparatus, reached a new record height of 27,200 feet (8,160 m).

Nevertheless, the achievements of the expedition were marred by a tragic accident. Seven Sherpas lost their lives in an avalanche on the North Col. The seven victims were left buried in the snow as their comrades wished. It was a terrible reminder that these pioneer expeditions were still somewhat ignorant of Himalayan conditions. At the time of the accident there had been a great fall of fresh snow and, as a member of the

Below: *One of the first oxygen sets being tested out in Tibet during the 1922 expedition. Expedition members, including George Finch (standing, right) look on with varying degrees of interest. Oxygen was a controversial feature of the 1922 expedition, and would remain a point of contention among climbers right through the 1930s. Many, like Mallory, objected to it, saying that such technology destroyed the spirit of mountaineering.*

expedition observed, seventeen persons on the North Col in such difficult, adverse conditions, was just fifteen too many.

Just before the expedition left for home, the Great Lama of the Rongbuk Monastery addressed them with these words:

The mountain will destroy you. The mountain has great powers and opens fissures in her side at will, and against such powers men have no strength.

He then revealed a new fresco, half historic, half prophetic, painted by his lamas on the portal walls of the monastery. This amazing picture showed the angered deity of the mountain surrounded by weird, wild dancing demons, white lions, barking dogs and hairy men. And at the foot, speared through and through, lay the naked body of a white man, who had dared to violate the sacred sanctuary of Chomolungma – Goddess Mother Of The World.

A year later, in 1923, Mallory accepted an invitation to lecture in the USA. During his tour he visited Boston and addressed the Appalachian Club. When it came to question time, a young lady in the audience asked him, "Why do you climb Mount Everest?" Mallory paused, and then made a reply that has been quoted by generations ever since: "Because it is there."

The Expedition of Legend

The next expedition took place in 1924 and is one that many people believed to be one of the finest for courage and tenacity ever mounted on this earth. It was also an expedition that was to become shrouded in mystery,

General Bruce was once more the leader with the ever faithful Captain Noel again in charge of the filming.

After months of magnificent endeavour, the climbing

Below: *Captain John Noel was the man in charge of the photographing and filming Bruce's 1922 expedition. He had been the first Westerner to sight Everest during his dashing trek through Tibet in 1913, and had been one of those who had inspired the first Reconnaissance expedition of 1921.*

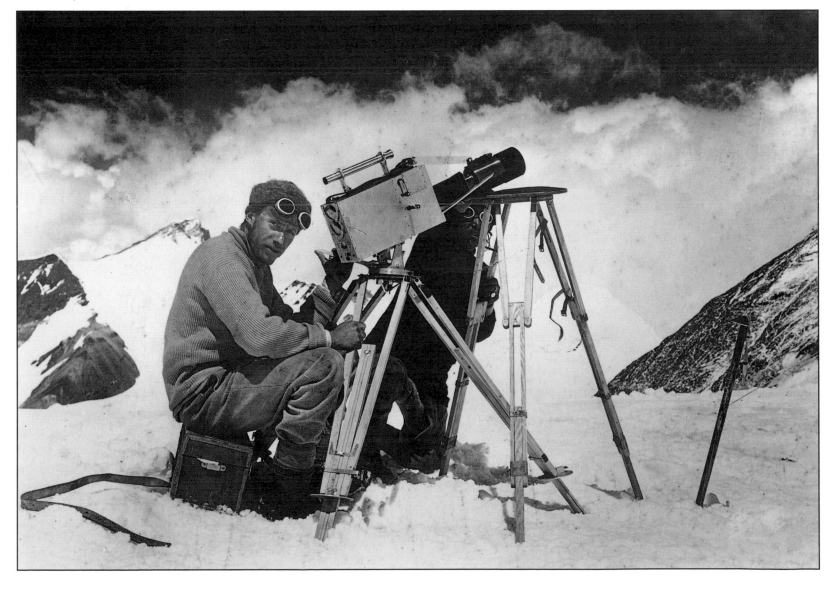

teams were still experiencing terrible hardship, as Everest blasted them with appalling weather conditions. Mallory wrote:

> The issue will shortly be decided. The third time we walk up the East Rongbuk Glacier, will be the last, for better or worse. We have counted our wounded and know, roughly, how much to strike off the strength of our little army, as we plan the next act of the battle. We expect no mercy from Everest . . . but yet it will be well for her that she deign to take notice of the little group that approaches stealthily over her glaciers again, and that she shall observe among the scattered remnants she has thrice put to flight, still a power to sting her very nose-tip. We are going to sail to the top this time and God with us – or stamp to the top with our teeth in the wind.

On 4 June, Colonel Norton and Dr Somerville reached 28,000 feet (8,400 m) without oxygen. At this point Somerville barely survived a desperate bout of breathlessness by forcing from his throat a piece of mucous membrane. Norton continued on to reach 28,126 feet (8,437 m), a new world record. Four days later on 8 June, the man they had nicknamed 'Sir Galahad', George Leigh Mallory, with his climbing companion, 22 year old Andrew Irvine set off from the highest camp at 27,000 feet (8,100 m) using the oxygen apparatus that Irvine had modified. Noel Odell, the support climber, arrived at 26,000 feet (7,800 m) on the same day and caught the last glimpse of Mallory and Irvine, going strong for the top:

> At 12.50, just after I had emerged in a state of jubilation at finding 'the first definite fossil on Everest', there was a sudden clearing of the atmosphere and then the entire summit ridge and the final peak of Everest were unveiled. My eyes became fixed on one tiny black spot silhouetted on a small snow crest beneath a rock step in the ridge and the black spot moved. Another black spot became apparent and moved up the snow to join the other on the crest. The first then approached the great rock step and shortly emerged at the top; the second did likewise. Then the whole fascinating vision vanished.

This sighting by Odell placed them at 28,250 feet (8,475 m) and still moving upwards towards the summit. Tragically, they were never seen again.

Above: *Were these two men the first to the summit? Portraits of George Leigh Mallory (left), and Andrew Irvine (right).*

Left: *From the expedition of 1922. Climbing the ice slope below the great crevasse on the North Col. The col had first been reached in 1921 by a three man party – and ten Sherpas – led by Mallory.*

Noel Odell concluded his report for the 1924 expedition with these words:

> The question remains. Has Mount Everest been climbed? It must be left unanswered, for there is no direct evidence. But bearing in mind all the circumstances I have set out above, and considering their position when last seen, I think myself there is a strong probability that Mallory and Irvine succeeded.

Tom Longstaff, who had been on the 1922 expedition wrote:

> It was my good luck to know them both, Mallory and Irvine: such splendid fellows, they got there alright. Somehow they were four hours late, but at 12.50 they were less than 800 feet (240 m) below and only a quarter of a mile away from the summit: Odell reports them moving quickly: therefore the oxygen was working well; nothing could have stopped these two with the goal well in their grasp at long last. It is obvious to any climber that they got up. It sounds a fair day: probably they were

Below: *Mallory and Irvine leaving Camp VI on the North Col for the last climb of their lives. Many years later, the writer and poet Robert Graves – who had climbed with Mallory – told Brian that the two men had exchanged hats before leaving camp. When asked why he said: "That's festivity Blessed".*

Below right: *Captain Noel in his 86th year, at his home in Brenzett, Romney Marsh, Kent. He is holding the camera he used during the expeditions of 1922 and 1924.*

above the clouds that hid them from Odell; how they must have appreciated the view of half the world; it was worth while to them; now they'll never grow old.

My fellow adventurers, these words "They'll never grow old" refer to the conjecture that people who die on Everest's snowy heights never age – not unlike the 5,000-year-old man who was discovered in the Alps recently.

By contrast to these two young climbers, Captain Noel lived until he was 99 years of age. During the last two years of his life I developed a delightful friendship with the 'Old Boy'. Sitting with him by the fireside of his home in Romney Marsh, late one afternoon, he talked of his feelings for Mallory and Irvine. Then suddenly he stopped and burst into tears. I wrapped my arms about him and cradled him like a baby. After a while he turned and looked at me, his ancient eyes red with weeping: "Tell me Blessed," he whispered. "If you had lived as they had lived, and died in the heat of nature, would you, yourself, wish for any better grave than the pure white snow of Everest?" The disappearance of Mallory and Irvine is a mystery. Long may it remain.

'The mountain reeked and smoked like a volcano; the embodiment of elemental fury'.

FRANK SMYTHE DESCRIBES THE STORMS OVER THE NORTH COL, 1933[2]

THE ATTEMPTS OF THE 1930s

AFTER THE FAMOUS expedition of 1924 there were no more attempts to scale the mountain in the Twenties. Ever determined and following the same route as their predecessors, the British made five attempts in the Thirties, starting in 1933 and finishing in 1938. In spite of these fine efforts by strong climbers like Frank Smythe, Eric Shipton, Wyn Harris and Lawrence Wager, they failed to get any higher than Captain Norton had done in 1924. There seemed to be a psychological barrier at 28,000 feet (8,400 m) that barred their way. Shipton said:

Everest defends itself with every means in its

power and its weapons are terrible ones; it is as exacting on the mind, as it is on the body. Those who tread its last thousand feet tread the physical limits of the world.

Those physical limits had an extraordinary effect on Frank Smythe in the spring of 1933. After a tremendous effort he found himself alone at 28,000 feet (8,400 m) with just sufficient energy left to descend to safety:

A strange feeling possessed me that I was accompanied by another. I have already mentioned a feeling of detachment in which it seemed as

Above: *A Tibetan crystal exorcising dagger, used in rituals to drive out evil spirits.*

Left: *The Base Camp of Eric Shipton's 1933 expedition, with Everest in the background. The camp is on the Central Rongbuk Glacier.*

Facing page: *The same glacier as seen from Everest's summit. Changtse (24,500 feet – 7,350 m) is in the foreground, with the desert plateau of Tibet beyond.*

though I stood aside and watched myself. It may be that the feeling that I was accompanied was due to the lack of oxygen and the mental and physical stress of climbing alone at altitude. This 'presence' was strong and friendly. In its company I could not feel lonely, neither could I come to any harm. Now as I halted and extracted some Mint Cake from my pocket, it was so clear and strong that I instinctively divided the mint into two halves and turned round with one half in my hand to offer it to my 'companion'."

After this experience Smythe descended several hundred feet and had his second experience.

Chancing to look over the North East Shoulder, now directly in front of me, I saw two dark objects in the sky. In shape they resembled kite balloons, and my first reaction was to wonder what on earth kite balloons could be doing near Everest; but a moment later I recognised this as an absurd thought. At the same time I was very puzzled. The objects were black and silhouetted sharply against the sky, or possibly a background of cloud. They were bulbous in shape, and one possessed what looked like squat, under developed wings, whilst the other had a beak-like protuberance, like the spout of a tea kettle. But what was most weird about them was that they distinctly pulsated with an in-and-out motion, as though they possessed some horrible quality of life. One interesting point is that these pulsations were much slower than my own heart-beats; of this I am certain and I mention it in view of a suggestion put forward afterwards, that it was an optical illusion and that the apparent pulsations synchronised with my pulse rate. After my first reaction of 'kite balloons' my brain seemed to function normally, and so interested was I that, believing them to be fantasies of my imagination, I deliberately put myself through a series of mental tests.

First of all I looked away. The objects did not follow my vision, but when my gaze returned to the North East Shoulder they were still hovering there. I looked away again and, by way of a more exacting mental test, identified by name a number of peaks, valleys and glaciers. I found no difficulty in Cho-Oyu, Gyachung Kang, Pumori and the Rongbuk Glacier, but when I again looked back the objects were in precisely the same position. Nothing was to be gained by further examination and I decided to carry on down. I was just starting

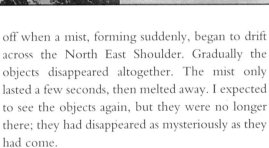

Far left: *The view north west from near Everest's Great Couloir, at about 28,000 feet (8,400 m).*

Left: *The first assault party of the 1933 expedition, Wyn Harris (left), and Lawrence Wager (right). These two men got to within 1,000 feet (300 m) of the summit.*

Below: *The slabs near the Great Couloir – the summit is on the left. The cross marks the highest point reached by the expedition. A modern view of the couloir can be seen on page 153.*

off when a mist, forming suddenly, began to drift across the North East Shoulder. Gradually the objects disappeared altogether. The mist only lasted a few seconds, then melted away. I expected to see the objects again, but they were no longer there; they had disappeared as mysteriously as they had come.

UFO experts today are quite convinced that Smythe witnessed alien spaceships. In contrast Doctor Raymond Greene, a member of the 1933 expedition, named Smythe's unidentified flying objects as 'Frank's pulsating teapots'!

If the 'kite balloon' phenomena was not enough, the 1933 expedition came up with another surprise. Descending from 28,000 feet (8,400 m), Wyn Harris and L.R. Wager arrived at Camp VI at 27,400 feet (8,220 m). This camp was occupied by Smythe and Eric Shipton. The first thing that Harris did was to fling down an ice axe at the entrance of the tent. "Found this", he said. "Must have belonged to Mallory or Irvine." The axe was found about 760 feet (228 m) below the crest of the North Ridge, 250 feet (75 m) east of the First Step at a height of about 27,700 feet (8,310 m). The axe lay on slabs at an angle of about 40 degrees, unsecured by either ledge or crack and dependant on friction alone for its

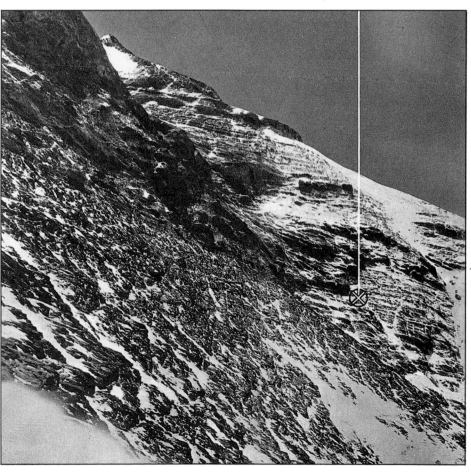

lodgement. It is astonishing that it should have remained there, for winds on Everest are known to exceed 100 mph (160 km/h). This discovery fuelled more speculation as to what happened to Mallory and Irvine. Theories have raged back and forth and round and round ever since.

Maurice Wilson's Story

In 1934, Everest's terrible weapons were unleashed on a brave eccentric Englishman called Maurice Wilson. He was born in Bradford, Yorkshire, in 1898, the third son of a self-made woollens manufacturer. On his 18th birthday he enlisted in the infantry in World War I and was commissioned a year later. At the third battle of Ypres he won the Military Cross. Shortly afterwards he was seriously wounded in his chest and left arm by machinegun fire and invalided home.

Wilson was over six feet (1.8 m) in height and as strong as a bull. Nevertheless, over the years he become physically ill, losing weight and racked by coughing spells. The medical profession had declared him incurable but to the amazement of his friends, he cured himself. His remedy consisted of fasting for 35 days, living only on sips of rice water and then, when the body was purged, of asking God to make him whole again. Wilson was a dedicated Christian. He had read about the 1924 expedition and was determined to succeed where they had failed, by climbing Everest on his own, and employing his method of fasting and divine faith to achieve it.

His story is astonishing and straight out of the realms of *Boys Own*. His plan was to fly to Everest and crash land on the East Rongbuk Glacier, and make his way to the summit on foot. All well and good! But he knew nothing about flying or climbing, so he set out to learn both.

He bought a Gypsy Moth aeroplane, three years old, which he named 'Ever-Wrest', and joined the London Aero Club. There he learned to fly and got his pilot's licence. He decided to teach himself to climb by trekking around the Lake District and Snowdonia in Wales for several weeks. Hardly ideal training for Everest! He bought such kit as he thought necessary for the mountain and on the 21 May flew off from Stag Lane Airfield, Edgware, bound for India and Everest. A short while before setting off, he tore up a last minute telegraph from the Air Ministry, forbidding the flight. There was no stopping this remarkable man. On and on he flew. Each country he arrived at had instructions from England to arrest him. They failed to do so for the simple reason that they couldn't help admiring him. For an inexperienced pilot to fly a second-hand Gypsy Moth to India was an amazing achievement in itself. The world's

press and the general public hailed him as a hero.

To cut a fine long story short, he miraculously succeeded in reaching the Rongbuk Monastery and after many weeks, in the company of three Sherpas, Tsering, Tewang, and Rinzing, slowly inched his way up the East Rongbuk Glacier.

The weather conditions were dreadful and blizzards constantly pinned them down and imprisoned them in their tents. Being utterly inexperienced in glacier travel, he had no idea which way to go. The Sherpas, though knowing the route, were themselves bewildered by the atrocious weather. Wilson hadn't a clue how to use his ice axe and wasted energy cutting useless steps. He records in his diary: "Eyes terrible and throat dry and sore, terrible when you can't put your head down for aching nerves."

He had to admit defeat and retreated back to the Rongbuk Monastery at 16,400 feet (4,920 m). Then, unbelievably, he went back up again and managed to get half way up the North Col to a height of 22,000 feet (6,600 m). Their position was now perilous and the weather was atrocious. By now the wise Sherpas had had enough and urged Wilson to give it up. He refused and they retreated several hundred feet to a lower camp to seek shelter. They were absolutely justified in doing so. Tewang and Tsering were desperately ill and under Rinzing's guidance, had done their utmost to look after Wilson. They felt that to continue in this manner was suicide. Wilson now had totally abandoned his idea of fasting and tucked into a Fortnum and Mason's food

Above: *The North Face of Everest, from above Camp V. The annotation shows Camp VI, the position where the ice axe from 1924 was found, and the highest point reached in the expedition. The Great Couloir is on the far right, and shows how Harris and Wager avoided Mallory and Irvine's route along the North Ridge and attempted instead to traverse across the North Face.*

Right: *The brave, but unfortunate aviator and solo climber, Maurice Wilson.*

Far right: *The Head Lama of the Rongbuk Monastery, in the 1930s.*

Top right: *The Rongbuk Monastery in 1922.*

dump left by the British 1933 expedition. Of course by now he knew the game was up! The recognition of the impossibility of his task started to sink in. In his diary his words became incoherent as despair set in. On 29 May he set off again and reached the foot of the North Col and camped there. On 30 May he stayed in bed and then on 31 May came the final entry in his dairy: "Off again, gorgeous day."

The body of Maurice Wilson was discovered by Eric Shipton's expedition the following year at a height of about 21,500 feet (6,450 m) at the base of the North Col. The body was lying on its left side with the knees drawn up. He was wearing a mauve pullover and grey flannel trousers with a woollen vest and pants underneath. There was a stove close to his left hand to which a guy-line to a tent was attached. The torn remnants of a tent were pulled out of the snow some few feet away from him. Shipton concluded that he must have died in his sleep of exhaustion and exposure inside his tent, the tent having been blown away at a later date. They found a

lightweight rucksack and a small Union Jack on which were the signatures of his girlfriends, and of course, his diary.

After a discussion, Shipton and his companions decided to bury Wilson in a crevasse. So they wrapped him in his tent and slid his body into the depths. The members of the 1935 British expedition raised their hats in respect and admiration. Shipton voiced the feelings of his party when he said of Wilson, 'We cannot fail to admire his courage'. Among this group of climbers was a Sherpa by the name of Tenzing Norgay who was later to become the most famous Sherpa of all time.

One would have thought that that was the end of Wilson's story. Not so! In 1960 a Chinese expedition came across his body, high up on the East Rongbuk Glacier. They too, like Shipton and his companions, lowered the body into a crevasse, feeling that was the end of it. They reckoned without Wilson. Even in death the determined, restless Yorkshireman seems to be a hard man to keep down. As the vast East Rongbuk Glacier moves relentlessly downwards a yard or two a day, moaning, twisting, and grinding anything in its path, his body periodically rises up in deathly defiance, as if still wanting to continue the struggle with Everest.

The renowned British climber, Roger Mear, was the last person to come across Wilson's body in 1989. Once more he was buried. Being a Yorkshireman myself, I can earnestly say that I sincerely hope that Wilson's bold Bradford bones will one day come to rest by the gentle temple of the Rongbuk Monastery.

THE FIRST FLIGHT OVER EVEREST

In the 1930s Everest remained unconquered. Therefore, it was felt that if a man couldn't climb it, how about flying over it? The isolation of the Himalayas and the violence and unpredictability of the weather, however, made any attempted flight an intimidating prospect.

Nevertheless, the British decided to give it a try. With backing from the Air Ministry, the Royal Geographical Society and Lady Huston, men and aircraft were organised and sent out to India, reaching their take-off point at Purnea, 150 miles (240 km) south of Everest on 22 March, 1933.

The aircraft chosen for the attempt was a Westland PV.3 bomber (the Houston Westland) powered by a supercharged Bristol Pegasus engine. In close support would be a Westland Wallace, while three de Havilland Moths would fly

Below: *Flying through the Himalayas for the first overflight of Everest in 1933. The cameraman Sidney Bonnet almost died during the flight when his oxygen feed pipe broke. His life was only saved by running repairs done with a handkerchief.*

reconnaissance. All the aircraft were biplanes. The Houston would be piloted by Lord Clydesdale and Lt. Col. Stewart Blacker, while the Wallace would be flown by Flt. Lt. David McIntyre, with cameraman Sidney Bonnet as observer.

On 3 April, at 8.25 am, after receiving reports of clear weather over the mountain, the two aircraft took off. To find their way they kept low, but approaching the Everest Massif they realised they did not have enough altitude to clear the summit. Trying to climb, the two planes were hit by a sudden downdraught which dropped them another 2,000 feet (600 m). Disaster was just averted as an updraft caught them in time. Clydesdale cleared the summit with only 500 feet (150 m) to spare. The time was 10.05. The two aircraft circled the summit for another 15 minutes before turning back.

TO THE SUMMIT AT LAST

CLIMBING ON EVEREST ceased during World War II. The war seriously weakened Britain, and its Empire was beginning to break up. Everest had always been known as 'The British Mountain' but now other nations had their beady eyes on it. Aware of this new competition, The British Alpine Club attempted to mount an expedition in 1947 and were told in no uncertain terms by the Viceroy of India, Lord Wavell, that permission to enter Tibet would be impossible. The Alpine Club was stunned. These were troubled times!

Then the unthinkable happened. The British Raj came to an end and the sub-continent was divided into two nations, India and Pakistan. Then, horror of horrors, most of the Himalayas were prohibited to outsiders. To make matters worse, the Dalai Lama had his horoscope cast that same year. It depressingly predicted that Tibet would be attacked by foreigners. Therefore, all foreigners were banned until 1950. Three years later, the Dalai Lama's horoscope proved to be horribly accurate.

In October 1950, a massive modern Chinese army invaded Tibet, attacking its frontiers in six places simultaneously. The ill-equipped Tibetan army could not possibly defend itself against such a mighty force. The Tibetan soldiers were gallant in the defence of their country, but the outcome was a forgone conclusion and the Tibetan army was routed.

Above: *A Tibetan bronze of the Buddhist protective deity Avalokitesvara.*

Left: *A view across Tibet prior to the Chinese invasion of 1950.*

Right: *The massive South West Face of Everest, first climbed by Chris Bonnington's 1975 British expedition, after six previous expeditions had failed. The 1975 climb included Doug Scott, Pertemba (Sirdar), Mick Burke and Pete Boardman. Mick Burke disappeared during a solo attempt for the summit, while Boardman was to die on the North East Ridge with Joe Tasker in 1982.*

The Dalai Lama

Out of interest the name 'Dalai Lama' used not to be used in Tibet at all. The great Mongolian ruler Altan Khan, who had embraced Buddhism, gave the title 'Dalai Lama' to the incarnations. Dalai Lama means literally, 'Broad Ocean'. Let me give you a few facts about the 'Holy Man'. His Holiness, the fourteenth Dalai Lama, Tenzin Gyatso, is the head of state and spiritual leader of the Tibetan people. He was born, Lhamo Dhondrub, on 6 July 1935, in a small village called Taktser in Northern Tibet. Born to a peasant family, His Holiness was recognised at the age of two, in accordance with Tibetan tradition, as the re-incarnation of his predecessor, the thirteenth Dalai Lama, and thus the incarnation of the Avolokitesvara, the Buddha of Compassion.

The Dalai Lamas are the manifestations of the Bodhisattva (Buddha) of Compassion, who chose to re-incarnate to serve the people. Lhamo Dhondrub was, as Dalai Lama, renamed Jetsun Jamphel Ngawang Lobsang Yeshe Tenzin Gyatso – Holy Lord, Gentle Glory, Compassionate, Defender of the Faith, Ocean of Wisdom. Tibetans normally refer to His Holiness as Yeshe Norbu, 'The Wish Fulfilling Gem' or simply Kundun 'The Presence'.

His enthronement ceremony took place on 22 February 1940 in Lhasa. At this time His Holiness received such names as 'The Tender Glorious One', 'The Mighty Of Speech', and 'The Excellent Understanding'. Although he was only five years old, everyone was astonished at the dignity of the child and the gravity with which he followed ceremonies that lasted for hours.

I was very fortunate to meet His Holiness in 1990 and I received his blessings, when I first attempted Everest's North Ridge in the same year. Give or take a month or two we are virtually the same age, yet our backgrounds

Below: *Thousands of Tibetan women surround the enormous Potala Palace in Lhasa to defend the Dalai Lama against the Chinese during the widespread Tibetan rebellion against their occupation. Soon fighting broke out in Lhasa and the Dalai Lama was forced to flee into exile in India.*

couldn't have been more contrasting. It is amusing to ponder that, when His Holiness was residing in splendour in his great Potala Palace in Lhasa as a God-King, I was learning to swim in a mucky canal in a mining village in South Yorkshire.

The Dalai Lama has displayed tremendous courage all his life. Just imagine the heavy responsibility that was placed on his shoulders on 17 November 1950. He was only 15 years old, when the massive Chinese army poured into his country and he was called upon to assume full political power, as head of state and government.

It was a sad day for Tibet and the presence of the Chinese invaders cast a dark shadow over the country. It was also a sad day for our mountaineers, as it was now impossible to approach Everest from the Northern side.

Nepal Opens

At the same time as the 'Dogs of War' howled their message of doom and gloom around the Himalayas, Nepal surprisingly opened up its frontiers and a whole new ball game presented itself. For courage and tenacity, the Nepalese are second to none, but it must have caused great concern in the capital, Kathmandu, to see the Chinese army advancing towards its northern borders. Nepal realised how isolated it was and immediately sought friends in the West. There was a revolution within the walls of the palace and the hereditary rulers, the Rana family, were removed. The King, who until then had been nothing more than a puppet, was given control of the country.

The opening of Nepal's borders to foreigners was a turning point in the history of Himalayan climbing. At last this fascinating, mystical kingdom welcomed, with open arms, the eager explorers of the West. It also gave climbers their first opportunity to take on many of the world's highest peaks, including of course, Everest. It was all so novel and exciting – a new country to experience and explore. The feeling of joy and relief was felt in every corner of the climbing world.

Oh! What mouth watering adventures this tiny kingdom offered! Zoologists, ornithologists and entomologists dreamed of unknown animals, birds and butterflies. Pilgrims from the West thirsted for the knowledge and wisdom of the Buddhist Lama's and to understand the

Above: *The flight from the Chinese invaders. The Dalai Lama is in the hand-carried palanguin on the left.*

Below: *His Holiness the 14th Dalai Lama, Tenzin Gyatso, born Lhamo Dhondrub 6 July, 1935, a reincarnation of the 13th Dalai Lama and thus an incarnation of Avalokitesvara, the Buddha of Compassion. His Holiness gives Brian his blessing in 1990.*

mysteries of incarnation, death and re-incarnation.

On the hillsides in unspoilt villages, in a region known as Sola Khumba, live the courageous, hardy, loyal and cheerful Sherpas. If you make a friend of one of them, you make a friend for life. Many people think the word Sherpa means 'Porter' or 'Guide'. This is a universal misapprehension. The Sherpas are a people, a tribe.

It is estimated that there are over one hundred thousand Sherpas in the high uplands of the Eastern Himalayas. Sherpa means 'Man of the East'. They are of Mongolian stock and long ago they migrated from Tibet. Like the Tibetans they are Buddhists.

The Himalayan Committee

Pre-war expeditions to Everest had been sponsored with money raised by an organisation called 'The Everest Committee' made up of members of both The Royal Geographical Society and The Alpine Club. They were now reformed and reconstituted as The Himalayan Committee. In 1951 this committee mounted a British reconnaissance expedition to Everest. The leader was Britain's most eminent mountaineer at this time, Eric Shipton – the same Shipton who had performed so splendidly in the pre-war expeditions on the Northern side. His team included M P Ward, T Bourdillon. W H Murrey and the New Zealanders E Hillary and H Riddiford. The Sirdar or Foreman was Angtharkay and Dr Dutt of the Geological Survey of India was also attached to the expedition. The cost of the reconnaissance was £2,500 and was largely met by granting exclusive coverage to *The Times*.

The objective was to explore the region around the Khumbu Glacier and find a possible way through the Ice

Above: *A Sherpa in the early 1950s. The term 'Sherpa' does not refer to the work done by these people as porters and climbers, but is a reference to their origins as a tribe. In Tibetan the name means man – or inhabitant – of the east.*

Right: *A view not seen by Westerners until the opening of Nepal in the 1950s. The South West Face of Everest framed between Lhotse on the right and Everest's own West Shoulder on the left, (which is not a separate mountain).*

Left: *A magnificent view of the Khumba Ice Fall tumbling out of the Western Cwm. Nuptse rears up on the right, Everest's West Ridge is on the left and the mighty presence of Lhotse is in the background. Surrounded as it is by these great mountain faces, avalanches are a threat on either side, so a climber has no other option but to risk going through the centre of the Ice Fall as the lesser of two evils.*

Facing page: *Sherpas carrying supplies to a higher camp, navigate their way towards pinnacles of ice about halfway up the Ice Fall. Nuptse overlooks them in the background.*

Fall to the Western Cwm beyond. The Western Cwm, by the way, was the name Mallory gave it, when he observed it from the Lho La in 1921. 'Cwm' is a Welsh word meaning a cirque or corrie.

This obstacle, the Ice Fall, filled all the mountaineers with dread at this time. An ice fall is exactly what the name implies. It is a region of ice that is falling, and though the movement is not generally visible to the eye, it is there none-the-less. It is estimated that the Khumbu Ice Fall on Everest moves three feet (.9 m) per day. It tumbles down over 2,000 feet (600 m) from the lip of the Western Cwm to an area just short of Base Camp at 17,500 feet (5,250 m).

The Khumbu Ice Fall

My friends, in 1993 I ascended this menacing and frightful place five times, which of course meant that I had to descend it five times also. It is not an experience that I would recommend to the faint hearted. There are thousands of 'ice falls' throughout the great mountain ranges of the world but none compares in notoriety to that of the Khumbu. It guards the approach to the Western Cwm and South Col of Everest and is one of its most formidable defences. Higher up the mountain problems of altitude, short wave ultra-violet rays, weather and technical difficulties can be met by human skill, but the Ice Fall presents the mountaineer with a sinister game of Russian Roulette. It brings into play a term that all mountaineers dread – 'objective danger'. It is a term that implies the kind of peril over which humans, however cautious, however experienced, can exert little control. The Khumbu Ice Fall is a frozen cascade of ice on a gigantic scale. Moving over a steep underlying bed of rock, the surface of the glacier is criss-crossed with open-mouthed crevasses and fallen blocks of ice, some as big as small skyscrapers.

Reliable-looking snow bridges have a nasty habit of disappearing suddenly into the depths. If you wish to climb Everest by the South Col route, then there is no escaping it. If you try and climb round its sides you will certainly be killed by enormous avalanches from the walls of Nuptse and Everest's West Ridge. There is no way around it! This giant staircase is the only way to the Western Cwm. Squeezed between the shoulders of Everest and Nuptse, it resembles a gigantic waterfall.

As I gazed at this terrifying obstacle, it so stirred my imagination that I half expected the snow and ice to melt and transform itself into a foaming, raging, roaring torrent of water, many times greater than the Niagara Falls. Fortunately the Ice Falls colossal strength has been restrained by 'Old King Cold'. But only restrained, for,

Above: *Base Camp situated just below the Ice Fall (Brian Blessed is standing second left.) The enormity and chaos of the Ice Fall rises off up into the distance. A line of prayer flags can be seen stretching off to the left immediately in front of the ice.*

though it may look totally immobilised, you can actually hear it, if you try, breathing and moving like a great white dragon. Its frustrations pierce the frosty air. The silence is broken by moaning and groaning, as its body quivers with the tons of ice that crush its black innards. With dark passion it grinds remorselessly downwards in its desire to crush all in its path. At night, when you are alone in your tent at Base Camp, the noises it emits play havoc with your nerves and frequently renders sleep impossible. In morbid curiosity you un-zip the flap on your tent, plunge your head into the freezing air and peer in the direction of 'The Dragon' in the hope that you might understand it and ease its pain.

In a full moon, the lunar-kissed peaks shine out like vast white giants. What stars! Stars of an autumn night on Mount Everest! The Milky Way, with its gracious curve enfolds the mountain in its dense tapestry of glowing

lights – lights of blue, gold, green, white, yellow and red. Orion and his outriders twinkle in the blanket of the night with their dazzling brightness. Rejoicing and cascading meteorites lend their brief fiery sparks to the heavenly scene, and Everest sleeps.

Not so 'The Dragon'. With eyes wide with insomnia, it glares down hungrily at the tiny figures in the tents at Base Camp. In the ghostly moonlight the scales of the monster take on a new aspect. The great blocks of ice are transformed into hundreds of ruined castles, their twisted towers and subterranean dungeons reverberate with the wailing voices of all the mortals who have perished there.

I am afraid that the Ice Fall's stunning beauty is wasted on me, for, as the ghosts of the night dissolve with the appearance of the dawn, they are replaced by the demons of the day.

Now the blazing semi-tropical sun pours down

through the thin air, and the labyrinth of ice turns into a furnace of remorseless heat, as it reflects the Sun's rays back at you and you are attacked by heat from above and below. There is no respite from this torture and climbers who, due to unforeseen circumstances, have been forced to descend it in the mid-day sun, emerge at the bottom like over-cooked loaves, their faces red like fire and greatly relieved that they have survived the ordeal. They sink in the snow by their tents at Base Camp and with burned throats and chapped lips they whisper thanks to the 'Goddess Mother of the Earth' for sparing their lives.

The awesome power of the Ice Fall commands respect. Every time the Sherpas prepare to ascend it, they perform a simple ceremony to Everest, which includes burning juniper, throwing rice and chanting the sacred mantra "Om Mani Padme Hum", (Hail, Jewel in the Lotus Flower). Whether the climbers are agnostics, atheists, or believers, they too join with the Sherpas and sing out the mantra with all their might. The moving sound of the ceremony blends with the roar of the avalanches and the groans of the Ice Fall and the whole scene takes on the epic grandeur of a Wagnerian opera.

Well, my friends, do you still want to climb Everest? Of course you do! And so did Eric Shipton's Reconnaissance in 1951.

On the 28 October 1951, Shipton and his whole climbing team, including the three Sherpas, Angtharkay, Nima and Pasang, forced their way through the Ice Fall and stood on the lip of the Western Cwm, at a height roughly judged to be about 20,600 feet (6,180 m). They then discovered that two enormous crevasses barred the way, and Shipton wisely decided to retreat to Base

Below left: *Brian returns from a descent of the Ice Fall 'with a face like an over-cooked loaf'.*

Left: *In a ritual of respect for the mountain, Sherpas prepare offerings and prayer flags before beginning an ascent. The ritual, undertaken before every climb, is known as the puja.*

Below: *Climbers cross a crevasse in the Ice Fall. Guide ropes and four ladders lashed together enable them to cross a chasm 100 feet (30 m) deep.*

Left: *As British Reconnaissance expedition of 1951 – led by Eric Shipton – trekked through the verdant wonders of Nepal, they saw country never before explored by Westerners. This is the view up to the pinnacle of the mountain Amadablam, on the way to Everest.*

Camp. After all, they were tired and stretched to the limit, and hadn't the materials or manpower to continue further. They had achieved their objective. Having ascended the Ice Fall, they had been able to observe at close quarters a clear route up the mountain. This route would involve bridging the two crevasses (which by the way are still there to this day), moving up the Western Cwm, ascending part of the Lhotse Face to the South Col and climbing on from there up the South East Ridge to the summit.

The Reconnaissance team had turned the key that unlocked the door to Everest. With this knowledge, the British could now happily assemble a full scale expedition in 1952 and attempt to climb Everest for the eighth time. Or could they?

The Swiss Go First

I'm afraid there was a slight hiccup! Someone hadn't done their homework! The Himalayan Committee, per-

haps over-confident that Everest was a British mountain, had not applied for permission for 1952 in time. It came as a horrible surprise to discover that there would be no expedition that year. The power of the magnificent Raj had ended and to add insult to injury a Swiss expedition had got in first! Really! The cheek of it! The Himalayan committee tried to retrieve the situation by requesting a joint expedition. A meeting was called and the committee, represented by Mr Basil Goodfellow, attended a meeting with the Swiss Foundation in Zurich on the 29 December 1951. From the start the terms offered to the Swiss were completely unacceptable. Goodfellow said that the committee were prepared to discuss partnership if the Swiss would accept being a group in a British expedition under Eric Shipton's leadership. The Swiss politely told the British Himalayan Committee to 'take a running jump' and announced that their plans for a pre-monsoon attempt were now complete. The Swiss also pointed out that they had been trying to get permission

Below: *Starting up the Western Cwm, with the avalanche-swept face of Nuptse behind. This point is at about 20,000 feet (6,000 m), and about an hours climb from Camp I.*

to attempt Everest since 1926 but had always been frustrated by British Imperial chauvinism. There was nothing for it, the British would have to sit it out and take this unwelcome news on their normally sporting chin.

At this time, the name Edmund Hillary began to appear more and more in the newspapers. Hillary was a tall, raw-boned bee-keeper, who lived in New Zealand. He had established himself as a fine climber with a superb physique. On the British Reconnaissance of 1951, he had been outstandingly the strongest. There was no doubt that he was a rising star.

Of course, we, the British public, viewing these events from afar, were genuinely fearful that the Swiss might climb Everest before we did. It was an understandable human weakness to feel this way, but nevertheless it would be awful, nay embarrassing, if the Swiss should climb it at their first attempt, when the British had lived through such a long line of glorious failures. Edmund Hillary himself put it in a nutshell:

> I think for the first time I was really admitting to myself quite honestly that I didn't want the Swiss to climb Everest. Let them get very high – good luck to them in that – but not to the summit! I wanted the summit left for a British party to have a crack at next year.

You can see that our emotions at the time were all churned up and confused to the point of bursting. But thankfully a voice, calm and clear, rang out and brought a much needed sanity to the proceedings. It belonged to Eric Shipton, who gently reminded us that the British and the Swiss had long had a special relationship and that, between them, they had practically 'invented' the sport of mountaineering. The British were always the brave amateurs; the Swiss, the professional guides; and the two nations combined magnificently to bring a delightful 'fizz' to the art of mountaineering.

Shipton made his way to Zurich. There he gallantly showed his Swiss rivals the photographs he had taken on the British Reconnaissance and magnanimously helped and advised them in every way.

Fortified by Shipton's advice, the Swiss leader, Rene Dittert, announced his team. They were a powerful force and the cream of Swiss climbers. Also, they were all good friends. Aubert, Asper, Chevalley, Flory, Hofstetter, Lambert, Roch and Vyss-Dunant. The remaining expedition members were scientists. Because of their kindness and friendliness, the Swiss were welcomed by the Sherpa people.

Left: *Trekking towards Everest with the Swiss expedition of 1952. This chain bridge, below the town of Charikot spans the Sun Kosi in Eastern Nepal. Everest is away to the north west. The expedition had to rely on bridges such as this one because the monsoon rains had made fords impassable.*

Right: *Everest from the Lhotse Face. Part of the Geneva Spur can be seen bottom right, with the South Col above it. The South West Face is on the far left. The route up the South East Ridge – which is the right hand skyline – is achieved by climbing up the snow fields to the left and reaching the ridge at its half way point. The ridge is then followed up to the summit.*

Raymond Lambert and André Roch were renowned throughout the world as outstanding mountaineers. The Sherpas' force numbered 20, led by none other than Tenzing Norgay, that same Tenzing who had climbed with Shipton and helped bury Wilson in 1935. If ever a man deserved to get to the summit of Everest, it was Tenzing. This was his fifth expedition to the mountain. He had been to Everest three times before with pre-war British expeditions.

Most of the Sherpas at the time still regarded mountaineering as simply a job. Not so Tenzing. He had the same driving ambition as any European climber. Already he had been to the top of the hard and dangerous sacred mountain, Nanda Devi East, 24,400 feet (7,320 m), with the French in 1921. There is no doubt at all that Tenzing impressed all who encountered him. Thirty eight years old, he weighed slightly over 10 stone (63 kg) and was quite tall by Sherpa standards. He possessed fine features with clear, twinkling eyes that reflected his kind ultra-sensitive nature. At times, particularly when gripped with curiosity, his open mobile face would assume a more serious and fixed expression. But soon this would evaporate to be replaced by his more usual infectious smile. Smile, smile, smile – he never stopped smiling. People were conscious of his teeth because of the smile. Yet if his smile softened the hearts of all who met him, then his eyes gladdened their souls.

He had been bewitched by the mountains since childhood. As a boy he used to go out with the yaks and wander free and alone along the mountain slopes. Many times he looked at Everest, rising high in the sky to the north, over the tops of the nearer mountains. But it was not known as Mount Everest to him. His mother had told him that it was called 'the mountain so high no bird can fly over it'.

As the years rolled by, he continued to climb along the slopes and rest his burning eyes on Everest. "No bird can fly over it", he mused. But what could a man do? A man with a dream. . . .

In 1952, he was a grown man and head Siddar on a Swiss expedition to Everest. Was the dream at last to become a reality? During the weeks that followed, Tenzing and his Sherpas built up a close, harmonious relationship with the Swiss. During the ascent of the Ice Fall the expedition leader, René Dittert, proved to be a jolly, lively individual, who hopped cheerfully from serac to serac and received the nick-name 'Khishigpa' – 'the flea' – from the giggling Sherpas. Raymond Lambert was already known by the Sherpas as 'Balu' – 'the bear' – as his appearance, when they approached the Western Cwm, closely resembled a bear. Working with the energy of ten men, he would frequently turn and grin at Tenzing and use his favourite expression – "Ça va bien" ("All goes well"). It was the beginning of a great

Previous pages: *Deep in the Western Cwm above Camp I (at about 20,000 feet – 6,000 m). Everest's South Face is on the left hand side, the South Col and Lhotse are ahead, and the North Face of Nuptse is on the right hand side.*

partnership. Tenzing greatly admired Lambert and the big Swiss returned the sentiment and roared aloud, "Tenzing, you have got three lungs. The higher you go, the better you get". "This is true", replied Tenzing and they both laughed. At 20,000 feet on the Western Cwm the expedition set up camp for the evening. Tenzing experienced a feeling of strength, warmth and happiness. "Yes" he thought. "Yes, I feel well, and it is going well". Perhaps this time, this time, at last, they would go on and on until the dream came true. Unfortunately, in his euphoria, he forgot Everest's unpredictability.

For the next two days, the weather was frightful and everyone suffered badly. But they pushed on through the Western Cwm and established Camp V at 22,640 feet (6,792 m) on the Lhotse Face. From here the route slanted diagonally upward following a deep couloir in the ice and then ran along a large outcrop of rock, which the Swiss named 'L'Eperon des Genevois', or 'the Geneva Spur'.

As in the Ice Fall, there had to be much trying and failing and long days of step-cutting and rope fixing. At this time Tenzing worked mostly with Lambert. By the beginning of the last week in May, all the preparations had been made and a supply dump had been established half-way up the South Col. Some of the climbers had been even higher, almost to the top of the Geneva Spur. Now the expedition was ready to try for the Col itself.

The team that was chosen to make the first effort to climb the Col and, if successful, to make the first attempt on the summit, consisted of Aubert, Flory, Lambert and Tenzing. They were joined by the Sherpas, Pasang Phutar, Phu Tharke, Da Namgal, Ajiba, Mingma Dorje and Ang Norbu. They tried to make a start on 24 May but were turned back by bad weather. Undaunted, they set off again the next day and this time kept going. The wind howled in derision and tore at their frail figures, threatening to hurl them two miles (3 km) down the Lhotse face to the Western Cwm below. Yet still they pressed on.

Toward midday they reached the half-way point at about 24,000 feet (7,200 m) and there added their own loads to the supply dump situated there. At this point Ajiba had a sudden attack of fever and had to descend. The rest divided his load and pressed on. This was no easy task for they were carrying tents, food, fuel and oxygen cylinders. Four hours later they reached the rocks of the Geneva Spur. The South Col was not far away but the sun was sinking and it was getting cold.

At this point, Ang Norbu and Mingma Dorje could go no further and dropped their loads and descended the face of the Lhotse to join Ajiba in the Western Cwm.

Again the rest of the party had to share the extra load, but this time they could only manage a small part of the extra weight. The rest would have to be brought up later. Amazingly, they carried on for a further two hours until it grew dark. At a point below the South Col, they stopped and dug out a platform in the steep snow and ice and set up two tents. The three Swiss struggled into one and the four Sherpas into the other. You can imagine their discomfiture. There they lay almost on top of each other. To make matters worse the temperature outside plummeted to 25 degrees below zero and the wind gathered momentum and buffeted their tents with terrible ferocity. Many times it seemed they would be blown away but somehow, miraculously, they survived.

The resourceful Tenzing provided his companions with a steady supply of soup and biscuits. They tried to sleep but it was too cold. Because of the temperature and the altitude (they were at over 25,000 feet – 7,500 m) exhaustion set in and some of the Sherpas feared that they would get frost bitten.

The Lhotse Face

In the autumn of 1993, I experienced at first hand the difficulties of ascending this daunting face. I was lucky; the weather was good and I had six marvellous Sherpas for company who wet-nursed me all the way. Yet at one point, a sudden blast of wind arose and compelled me to put on my outer fleece-lined gloves. The whole action took only three minutes, yet within that short space of time I experienced intense pain in my hands from the sudden drop in temperature. The pain was indescribable! There I was, a big healthy man reduced to a whimpering baby by the cold. There was no danger that I would fall, although I was on a 60 degree slope, because I was anchored to the rope with my Karabiner sling and trusty Jumar. But I must have looked like a demented spider as I thrashed about, trying desperately to bring some feeling back to my unresponsive fingers.

I tried every position you could imagine – up my crutch, under my arm-pits! After ten minutes, I let out a howl of relief as the first signs of life returned. The sudden surge of blood back into my fingers resulted, of course, in yet more agony and I continued to whine like a child until the pain subsided and I could resume jumaring up the rope.

I describe this because I want to give you some idea of their suffering. For what I experienced was as nothing to what the Swiss and their Sherpas endured.

The weather conditions were appalling. The clothes and technical equipment that we have today is infinitely superior to anything they possessed at that time. They

were also carrying loads that were over 40 lbs (16 kg) in weight on a gigantic, steep, snow and ice slope at between 22,000 and 26,000 feet (6,600 and 7,800 m) and they were without the use of oxygen. What little oxygen they had was needed for the final summit push from the South Col. Above all they were treading new ground! It was all unknown. In 1993, we were following in the footsteps of numerous expeditions that had ascended by the South Col route. Apart from the odd deviation, every foot of the way is well known – very reassuring in such a hostile environment. What doubts and fears must have haunted their cold and paralysed heads in 1952. Would the effort of getting up to the South Col leave them too weak to progress up the South East Ridge? More to the point, would the effort leave them too weak to descend or survive? What would the conditions be on the Col? From their observations lower down, they had seen that the winds there could attain speeds of over

100mph (160k/mh). Yet no doubt, alongside their fears, must have been a feeling of great pride and exhaultation, for they were pioneering a route up the highest mountain on God's Earth.

The night of the 25 May seemed to last for ever. Then at long last it was morning and, thank God, it was a still, clear morning. They looked up and realised that the Col was very close. They would reach it that day.

Only four of the party started up – Lambert, Aubert, Flory and Tenzing. The three Sherpas, Phu Tharke, Da Namgyal and Pasang Phuter went down to bring up the loads that had been left below at the supply dump. At about 10.00 a.m. the Swiss and Tenzing reached the South Col and celebrated the great moment with huge bear hugs. While the Swiss set about unpacking and erecting tents, Tenzing descended to meet the other Sherpas and to help them carry up the loads. He had hoped to meet them part way down but was surprised to

Above: *Camp II in the Western Cwm, with the enormous Lhotse Face in the background. This image foreshortens the Face, which is in fact 6,000 feet (1,800 m) high and takes the climber from 22,000 feet (6,600 m) to nearly 28,000 feet (8,400 m). Camp III is located a third of the way up the Face at 23,500 feet (7,050 m).*

The centre of the Face shows the signs of a massive avalanche of fresh monsoon snow 20 feet (6 m) deep, and 1,600 feet (500 m) wide. This is prime avalanche terrain.

find that they had still not left the half-way mark at the bivouac supply dump. Pasang Phuter was lying helplessly in his tent, claiming that he was too ill and was about to die. "No, you are not," said Tenzing. "You are going to be alright. You are going to get up and carry a load to the South Col."

Pasang would not listen and informed Tenzing that he was now dead. Tenzing swore at him and began slapping and kicking him to prove he wasn't dead. He told Pasang that if the loads did not get up to the Col, the three Sahibs would surely die, adding that if he left Pasang where he was, he, too, would surely die – and this time not only in his imagination. There was still no response from Pasang so Tenzing yelled at him, "Come on! Come on Jockey!" The Sherpas had nicknamed Pasang 'Jockey' because he was little and often used to ride horses at Darjeeling race track. This appeal got him to his feet and out of the tent. The four Sherpas then slung on their loads and started.

They huffed and puffed and crawled and staggered until they finally reached the South Col. By this time Phu Tharke and Da Namgyal were almost as exhausted as Pasang and barely had the energy to creep into their tents.

The amazing Tenzing, descended twice more to the supply dump and brought up more food and equipment. That evening, after consuming as much liquid as possible, they all nestled into their sleeping bags and prepared for their first night on the South Col.

The South Col

What is the South Col? Bear with me as I once again leap forward to the year 1993 – 8 October 1993 to be precise. On that exciting day I found myself on the Col in the company of three Sahibs and three Sherpas. From our high camp at 23,500 feet (7,050 m) on the Lhotse Face, we had climbed up the ice slopes and yellow rock band, up the Geneva Spur and onto the Col at 26,200 feet (7,860 m). During the ascent our legs had protested, our lungs had protested and our minds had protested. But, as we reached the Col, something beyond our legs and lungs and minds functioned deep within us. For the misery and pain seemed to disappear as we embraced in tearful celebration. We were deeply moved and profoundly relieved to have arrived safely, for the monsoon conditions in the Himalayas that year were reported to be the worst in living memory.

I have been in many wild and lonely places in my life but nothing compares to the South Col on Everest: "Like being on the moon", said one climber. It is a barren, hostile plateau, lying between the final peaks of

Everest and Lhotse. In the spring, the surface of this wasteland is partly covered with stones and partly covered with sheets of glittering white and blue ice. In the autumn, when we were there, it was covered in a deep carpet of snow.

The size of Lords Cricket Ground, it is a place that is alien to mankind. At such great heights, the thin air gives no protection against the severity of the sun's power.

Left: *The South Col on the skyline at 23,500 feet (7,050 m) seen from the Lhotse Face. The Geneva Spur can be seen rising from right hand centre. Lhotse itself rises up on the right hand side. The sheer exposed nature of the South Col makes it a very dangerous place.*

Down pour the deadly short-wave ultra-violet rays. The ice crystals shimmer with a haunting beauty. You are living in the world of the dead. At that altitude the simple action of pulling on your plastic boots makes your heart beat like a hammer against your rib-cage. Though painful, this produces the strange but positive feeling that you are more alive than at any other time in your life. But you are deluding yourself. After three or four, possibly five days without oxygen – you die, for the simple reason that you are too high. Too high for even a helicopter to rescue you.

As for the views, they defy description. The written word, however inspired or carefully chosen, cannot convey the beatific beauty of the landscape up there. On one side is great Lhotse with its amusing 'teddy bear ears' and on the other, majestic Everest, with its summit streamer of ice particles fluttering away like a white banner on a colossal battleship. On, on, float the Himalyas for hundreds of miles on a sea of white, pink and turquoise clouds. Each giant mountain soars upwards into the cobalt-blue sky. They have an aura of invincibility. Yet despite the intoxicating scenery, you cannot but be aware of the fearful wind that brings a sense of dread into your heart. The wind is a real killer and there are several corpses lying around on the Col that serve as a grim reminder of its destructive power. You simply have to get out of its way as quickly as possible. It chills and depresses and debilitates. It also seems capable of penetrating the most advanced clothing invented by man. The wind on that place is the most savage and cruel in the world.

They say that it is westerly but it seems to hit you from every direction. The expression 'open to the four winds' might have originated there. Round and round it goes, and up and down. It is invisible. Your hope of survival lies in detecting where its voice comes from, for it shrieks and rumbles and howls with the ferocity of a thousand banshees. Then for a few moments there is a sudden lull and you can hear the silence.

Gradually, from a distance, you hear a sound like several express steam engines approaching. In cold fear you brace yourself for the dreaded onslaught. Like a cat teasing a mouse, the sound seems to weaken in intensity and assumes an almost pleasant, fragile, moaning quality. It circles tantalisingly around for several seconds until, with gathering momentum, it vents its pent up rage on the stoical surface of the Col and its puny inhabitants, both dead and alive. It pulverises the Everest Massif with waves of irresistible cold and you hold on to your tent for grim death and pray that you have done a good enough job in battening down. If you are fortunate, after several hours the wind desists and goes off to plague some other region. Towards morning, after a sleepless night, you pop your weary head out of your sleeping bag and discover that it, and the interior of the tent, is covered in freezing powder snow and you wonder what the hell you are doing there.

I can only hope that that gives you some idea of what the Swiss and the Sherpas had to put up with in 1952.

On the morning of 27 May, the three Sherpas, with the exception of Tenzing, were completely worn out. Pasang 'Jockey' was still convinced he was dead and Phu Tharke and Da Namgyal begged Tenzing not to attempt to go any higher.

After a lengthy discussion Tenzing managed to get Jockey to his feet. He tied him tightly on the rope between Phu Tharke and Da Namgyal and the three of them started down. The three Swiss and Tenzing made preparations to go up.

Without the others to help with the loads, they could not carry nearly enough for the next high camp and any prospect of gaining the summit seemed remote. But off they went – Aubert and Flory on one rope and Tenzing and Lambert on the other. On and on they climbed, hour after hour. It was all new territory. With heads bowed and backs breaking, they moved up the Col, along the steep snow slope, to the base of the South East Ridge and then onto the Ridge itself.

It was a colossal labour! They had only one tent between them, which Tenzing carried. They each also carried a small tank of oxygen but the oxygen, instead of being beneficial, proved an added burden. The apparatus would only work when they were resting or standing still. It meant that they had to carry the oxygen bottles without getting any benefit whilst actually climbing. The apparatus was so primitive that it was less effective than the system used by the British in the 1920s. In retrospect, they would have been better off had they dumped it and climbed without oxygen. But, remarkably, on they went and reached 27,000 feet (8,100 m). Tenzing was thrilled. "I have broken my own record," he whispered to Lambert. "I am higher than I was at Camp VI on the other side of the mountain in 1938."

There were still two thousand feet to climb but the 'Goddess Mother of the Earth' was smiling on them at long last, for the weather was calm and the sky was clear.

At about 27,500 feet (8,250 m) Tenzing spotted a small level place where the tent could be pitched. Flory and Aubert joined them and the three Swiss discussed the situation. It was decided that Flory and Aubert should go down and Lambert and Tenzing would stay. There was only one tent and little food, and the two Swiss made the decision without any fuss. It was an emotional moment and, with tears in their eyes, Aubert and Flory slapped the backs of their companions. "Take care of yourselves," they said and departed. When they had disappeared from sight, Tenzing and Lambert laboriously pitched the little tent.

The evening was so calm they were able to sit outside in the fading sunlight. There they were, two fine men from entirely different nationalities – the man of the east and the man of the west, sitting together in perfect harmony and united in the quest to climb the highest mountain in the world. "Tomorrow," said Tenzing, "You and I climb to the summit."

When it grew dark and colder, they crawled into their tent. They had no stove and ate a little cheese, which they washed down with snow that they melted over a candle! They must have been terribly dehydrated and they had no sleeping bags. With the intense cold of the night penetrating the walls of the tent as if it were tissue paper, their situation was hazardous to say the least. They dared not sleep for fear they would not wake up again. They spent hours slapping and rubbing one another to keep their circulation moving.

In the blackness of the Himalayan night, these two vulnerable souls, rubbed, rubbed, rubbed and slapped, slapped, slapped, and grimly grinned, as they sucked feverishly, like new born babies, the life-giving drops that fell reluctantly from the heated hard snow. Hour after hour passed until, at last, the faint streaks of dawn lit up the white frosted tent. They were still alive. They had survived.

The Final Push

Stiff and frozen to the marrow, they emerged from their tent and tried to focus their bleary red eyes on the landscape before them. What they saw was not good. The weather had deteriorated. Dense clouds filled the sky and the wind was beginning to rise. Nevertheless Lambert jerked his thumb at the ridge and with a wink said once more, "Ça va bien."

An hour later they were on their way. They had three tanks of oxygen between them but, as before, they were of no use whilst moving and after a while they dropped them to relieve themselves of the weight. Every 20 yards (18 m) or so they changed places, so as to share the harder work of breaking the trail. They frequently found themselves up to their waists in snow and the wind grew in intensity and peppered their faces with ice.

Three hours went by and their progress became painfully slow. The climb itself was technically not too hard but they were desperately tired. On one side of the

ridge was a great precipice and on the other, a cornice of snow overhanging a great void, which, if they were not careful, would plunge them into the black hole of eternal night.

Tenzing's throat was horribly sore and dried up and he was aching with thirst. Even his renowned 'third lung' was failing him. The two men frequently had to crawl on all fours in the deep snow and had constantly to check their position in the worsening weather conditions.

From time to time waves of cold mist enveloped them and forced them to remain motionless and frozen until it passed away and they could once again see the route. They were climbing without oxygen, without food and water, and they were slowing down because of the debilitating effect of dehydration. This condition was now

Below: One of the pioneers of Himalayan exploration. Eric Shipton just before leaving for his climb of Cho-Oyu in 1952. The peak, at 26,857 feet (8,057 m) was meant to be dress rehearsal for Everest the following year. The failure of the expedition, however, led to questions being asked about Shipton's style of leadership.

Left: *The irrepressible smile of the man who would attempt Everest seven times, and would eventually succeed. Tenzing Norgay.*

cal feet [195 m], Lambert reckoned later; and it had taken us five hours. I looked up and there was the South summit about 500 feet [150 m] above us. Not *the* summit, just the South summit, and beyond it . . . I believe in God. I believe that in men's hardest moments He sometimes tells men what to do and that He did then for Lambert and I. We could have gone further. We could perhaps have gone to the top. But we could not have got down again. To go on would be to die . . . and we did not go on. We stopped and turned back . . . we had reached an altitude of about 28,250 feet [8,475 m] . . . the highest men had ever climbed in the world. But it was still not enough. We turned without speaking. We descended without speaking. Down the long ridge, past the high camp, along the ridge again, along the snow-slope. Slowly – slowly, down – down – down. That was all for Lambert and me.

The Swiss Try Again

The news of the failure of the Swiss brought a national sigh of relief in Britain. But this euphoria quickly turned to consternation, when it became known that the Swiss intended to have another crack at the mountain in the autumn. After all, 1952 belonged to them. They had permission for the entire year and they realised that this might be their last chance, as the next year was the turn of the British and, after them, the French. It would be 1956 before they would have another opportunity and it seemed unlikely that the mountain would hold out much longer.

It was the first time any nation had made two attempts in one year. The chances of climbing Everest in the post-monsoon period – the autumn – had been debated for many years.

But the Swiss tried – and failed. The savage cold and high winds overtook them and they got no higher than the South Col. Tragically, the Sherpa Mingma Dorje was killed by falling ice on the Lhotse Face. Nevertheless, it was a tremendous performance by the Swiss in 1952 and the world saluted them.

In London in 1952, pressure on the Himalayan Committee for success in 1953 was overwhelming. Britain had a new Queen. She was to be crowned in Westminster Abbey in June 1953. The ascent of mighty Everest would make a wonderful Coronation gift. Would this not majestically herald in a new Elizabethan age? In everyone's minds it was a forgone conclusion that the leader of the expedition would be Eric Shipton. In 1952, he probably had a greater knowledge of the moun-

raising the concentration of red cells in their blood stream. The increased number of cells made their blood thicker and more difficult to move, and caused an unevenness of flow in their small blood vessels. They were now high in the 'death zone' and at the limits of physical endurance. They were approaching 28,000 feet (8,400 m).

After two more hours of crawling, groaning and gasping for air, the magnificent Lambert turned and grinned and said for the umpteenth time: "Ça va bien." To which Tenzing answered back, "Ça va bien." But it was not true. It was not going well and both men knew it.

Tenzing began to think of his home and family. The fate of Mallory and Irvine also crossed his mind and his serious features set in concentration. We might get to the top, he thought, but will we get down? Severe prolonged oxygen depravation of the cerebellum, that part of the brain that controls muscular movement, began to affect their bodies and compelled them to rest for long periods of time. They would move and stop, move again, and stop again. This is how Tenzing remembered the end:

Then we stopped and did not move again. Lambert stood motionless, hunched in the wind and driving snow and I knew he was working things out. I tried to work them out too but it was even harder to think than to breathe. I looked down. We had come – how far? About 650 verti-

tains of central Asia than any man under the sun. As well as taking part in many expeditions in the 1930s on such peaks as Everest, Kamet, Nanda Devi and in the Shaks Gam, he had been British Consul in both Kash Gar and Kunming.

Eric Shipton

Shipton was undoubtedly Britain's most eminent mountaineer at this time and he had established himself, with Bill Tilman, as an outstanding explorer as well. Yet these impressive credentials did not fully convince the British Himalayan Committee that he was the right man for the job.

There was some justification for the committee to feel this way. Shipton was more 'mountain explorer' than 'technical climber'. For him, reaching the top of a mountain was just part of the experience and not an end in itself. Shipton admitted this to the committee himself, and stated that he thought a younger man might be better suited to the role. The committee must have been impressed and, at the same time, confused by Shipton's honesty. It was hardly the fighting-talk of a determined leader. Was this the 'man of destiny' that they were seeking – the man who would lead his troops through the dangers of the Ice Fall, the rigours of the Western Cwm and the Lhotse Face – the leader, who could negotiate the intimidating South Col and South East Ridge and reach the summit of Everest itself?

There is no doubt at all that the redoubtable Shipton had the skill, experience, bravery and proven qualities of leadership for such an enterprise; but was his heart in it? This was Britain's last chance. If we didn't climb it this time, the Swiss were bound to succeed in their next attempt in 1956. The urgency of the situation transmitted itself to all, who were obsessed with this great quest.

Yes, we all expected Eric Shipton to be named leader. Then lo and behold, out of the blue, the Himalayan Committee announced that they had appointed Major John Hunt as leader of the expedition.

"John who?" everyone asked. The public had never heard of him. There was an angry reaction to the 'sacking' of Shipton. A powerful young climber called Tom Bourdillon, who had been to Cho-Oyu and was the oxygen expert on the coming expedition, was so upset that he offered his resignation. Badly shaken as he was by the turn of events, Shipton nevertheless found the energy to persuade Bourdillon to change his mind.

Over a period of time, the Committee's decision was accepted and the clouds of dissent gradually disappeared, to be replaced by a strong feeling of optimism. This must be attributed to Major John Hunt himself.'

Organising the 1953 Expedition

Hunt was able to weld his disparate climbers into a particularly happy team. He organised the expedition with quiet, unerring efficiency. He brought a military precision and a genius for organisation to the enterprise. One commentator, Ingrid Cranfield, in a profile of Hunt summed him up in this way:

> To Hunt, an 'assault' on the mountain merely meant a concentrated, military style operation: whereas to Shipton 'assault' sounded more like a criminal offence.

To some extent I think this comment by Cranfield is rather misleading. Hunt held strong Christian beliefs and

Right: The Himalayan Committee's decision not to select Shipton as leader of the 1953 British expedition caused an outcry. However, they would be vindicated in their choice of Colonel John Hunt, a man with the will and a genius for organisation great enough to crack mountaineering's biggest challenge.

I gather from his writings that his approach to climbing was essentially romantic. His love of adventure seems to me to stem from a clear belief in God. He also has a marvellous ability to write vividly about his numerous adventures and I admire him greatly both as an author and an artist.

Hunt officially took up his duties as leader on 9 October 1952. He had only five months to organise the expedition – a mammoth task! By 5 November he had produced a series of papers which were a detailed draft plan of how best to tackle Everest and give every chance of success. Any doubts about his leadership were now dispelled. This man matched the hour.

Had the British been granted permission to climb Everest in 1952, instead of the Swiss, they would not, in

Below: *Getting the expedition to the mountain would be Hunt's first task. This is a camp at Dingboche, Nepal on the expedition's trek towards Everest.*

all probability, have been ready to mount an assault. Very little equipment had been tried out on the Reconnaisance in 1951 and there was still a great deal of work to be done on the important oxygen equipment.

The Oxygen Debate

The use of oxygen on Everest's Northern side in the Twenties and Thirties had in general proved ineffective. The apparatus used by the Swiss in 1952 was a disaster. They used closed-circuit oxygen sets. The advantage of this system is that it re-cycles the oxygen, thereby doing away with the need to carry large numbers of cylinders, and so the Swiss apparatus weighed only 5¼ lbs (2 kg). Though it worked perfectly at lower altitudes, the climbers discovered that above 23,000 feet (6,900 m) the

Above: *An oxygen set of the type used by British expeditions of the 1930s. The use of such an artificial aid to climbing still divided mountaineers. The ascent in 1933 took several sets, but only used them for research, though the expedition in 1938 used them to good effect above the North Col.*

Above right: *Jinette Harrison just below the summit during her successful ascent in 1993. The oxygen set she wears is of Russian origin and is considered one of the best available. It uses an open system, as do all oxygen sets today.*

resistance of the valves was too great. A positive effort was needed to breathe.

Dr LGC Pugh (Griff to his friends) of the Medical Research Council emphasised the importance of making the right choice of oxygen equipment. Hunt appointed Peter Lloyd, who had been a member of the 1938 expedition, to take charge of this vital decision. Lloyd was assisted by the climber Tom Bourdillon and Alf Bridge. The first two had scientific expertise and Bridge was an engineer working for the Gas Board.

Bourdillon had been working to develop the closed-circuit oxygen system. In this system, a chemical exchange took place between the carbon-dioxide breathed out by the climber and a cylinder of soda-lime, which had the effect that oxygen was returned to the system for use over and over again. A supply of fresh oxygen replaced what was actually absorbed by the climber's body, and so obviously the wastage rate was much reduced and less oxygen needed to be carried. From time to time the soda-lime cartridge became exhausted but this was easily replaced by a quick-loading cartridge system. A second benefit of the closed-circuit was that it provided a richer oxygen supply. The drawback of the Bourdillon system was that it was very new and scarcely beyond the prototype stage.

In contrast, the other oxygen system, the open-circuit, operates on the principal that the climber breathes predominantly the air around him but it is enriched by a small percentage of pure oxygen. This method possesses the great advantage of simplicity and reliability, though of necessity it supplies a lower concentration of oxygen to the climber than does the closed-circuit system.

Peter Lloyd certainly distrusted the closed-circuit system when he wrote:

My own experience in 1938 on Everest when I had done comparative trials on the open- and closed-circuit systems had led me to distrust the closed-circuit design with its inherent complexity and with the inevitable resistance to breathing caused by the duct and valve gear . . . it is inherently too claustrophobic and complex and that is why it has never caught on!

When I was on the northern side of Everest in 1990, several climbers told me that the oxygen mask had filled them with a feeling of claustrophobia and this despite the fact that they had been using the more friendly, natural open-circuit system.

In 1993 I reached my high point on Everest at 27,800

OXYGEN SETS

The oxygen set of the type used in the British expeditions of the 1920s was a heavy and cumbersome piece of equipment. Four steel cylinders were held in a Bergen pack frame. Together with tube, valves and face mask the whole apparatus when full weighed 32 lbs (14.5 kg).

In 1922 the sets were supplied with two types of face mask. One used valves, which in practice proved useless, if not dangerous, to the wearer. The other was a simple copper and chamois leather affair covering an open oxygen pipe. The mask was bent to fit the climber's face, and oxygen flow was regulated by the wearer's teeth.

The sets were designed to supply sufficient oxygen to simulate an altitude of 15,000 feet (4,500 m) in the climber's body. However, the effects of altitude were still little understood in these early years and much of the work with oxygen was influenced by pure theory, sheer guesswork – and in the case of many traditionally-minded climbers – blind prejudice.

For the 1922 expedition, ten sets of apparatus were constructed and sent, but due to the rough journey overland only three actually worked by the time the expedition reached the mountain.

The oxygen sets used in the 1953 expedition were altogether different. Designed and built with the knowledge and experience gained by earlier high-altitude climbs, as well as the technologies developed in high-altitude aviation. Alloy cylinders and aluminium frames kept the weight to 29 lbs (13 kg), not a great deal lighter than the sets in 1922, but they were more efficient and could supply over three times more oxygen.

While the arguments over the propriety of using oxygen had been won by this time, the question of whether a system should close or open was still being debated. The expedition of 1953 compromised and took both systems. The failure of the first assault by Evans and Bourdillon – who were using closed sets – and the success of Hillary and Tenzing – who used the open system, settled the debate in the latter's favour and ensured that the open oxygen system is the one used today.

A major innovation of the 1953 expedition was the use of a separate oxygen system designed for use while climbers slept. It was a simple innovation consisting of 'T' connector feeding two masks from one cylinder. The object was to give the climbers better rest at night.

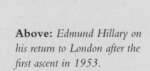

Above: *Edmund Hillary on his return to London after the first ascent in 1953.*

Left: *George Finch's oxygen set, as used during the 1922 expedition.*

Right: *The open-circuit oxygen equipment used by the 1953 expedition.*

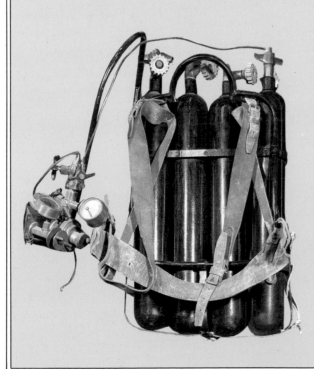

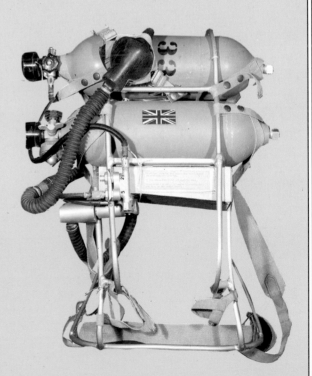

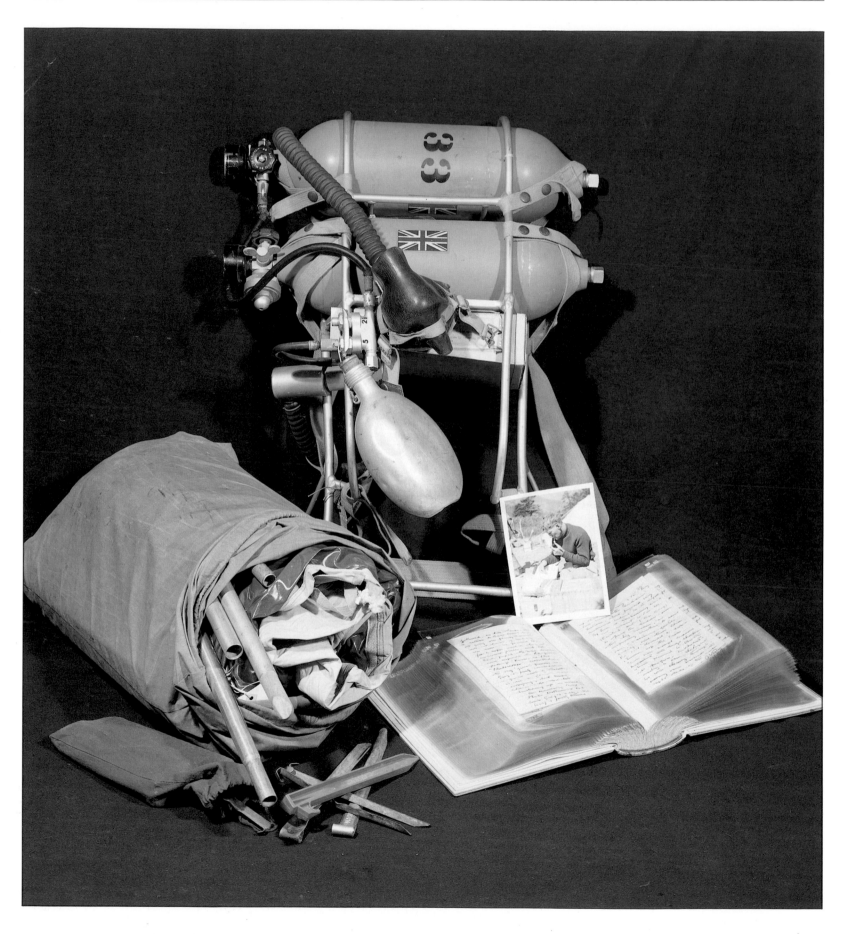

feet (8,340 m) without oxygen. But I have tried on masks at Base Camp and have found that they give me a feeling of being cut-off from my surroundings. If I had been using oxygen on the expedition, I would certainly have preferred to use the open-circuit system, because I would have felt, at least to some extent, part of the environment: I would have been breathing naturally to some degree, and only partially using artificially enriched air. Also you can increase the flow of oxygen, say from one litre to six litres per minute, depending on the difficulty of the terrain and your physical condition.

When you climb Everest's South side, you must be perfectly acclimatised to reach the South Col at 26,200 feet (7,860 m), if possible without the use of oxygen, though this is not strictly necessary. When you start to move upwards to the summit at 29,028 feet (8,708 m) from the Col, if you are using the open-circuit system, you are still, I feel, acclimatising to some degree. If for some reason the apparatus should break down close to the summit, this acclimatisation would give you a fine chance of surviving and getting down. With the closed-circuit system the risks would be much greater. When using this system, you breathe 100 per cent pure oxygen. The exhaled air is re-circulated past a chemical absorbent, for removal of carbon dioxide, which provides you at 29,028 feet (8,708 m) with a pressure of oxygen equivalent to that attained breathing at sea level. You are likely to start using oxygen from between 22,000 (6,600 m) and 23,500 feet (7,050 m). If your apparatus malfunctioned near Everest's summit, you would be literally like a 'fish out of water'. Make no mistake, you would be in deep, deep trouble. Your chances of survival would be minimal. It doesn't bear thinking about.

The Decision

In 1952, the Bourdillon apparatus had its supporters on the committee and in the end it was decided that 12 open and eight closed sets would be taken.

Numerous RAF open-type sets would also be taken for training, sleeping, spares, etc. Dr Griffith Pugh, the physiologist, played a very important part in the preparations. Food for the expedition was carefully worked out and the equipment, with specially designed 'high-altitude' boots, tenting and clothing was better than anything that had been used before. Each climber was provided with Shell clothing consisting of anorak and over trousers of a close-woven material made of cotton warp and nylon weft, which weighed only 4¾ozs (32 g) per square yard but which was utterly impervious to winds up to 100 mph (160 km/h). It was proofed with

'Mystolen' to make the garments showerproof.

Hunt wanted a team that would work together in harmony. He restricted membership to men from Britain and the Commonwealth. He appreciated as much as any man the special interest that geologists, botanists and naturalists had brought to previous expeditions, but on this venture, such activities were completely ruled out. Every member of this expedition would contribute directly to the climbing.

He settled on a large and impressive team; 12 climbers and 36 high-altitude porters. The 12 climbers were: Tom Bourdillon, George Band, Charles Evans, Alfred Gregory, John Hunt, Michael Ward, Edmund Hillary, Wilfred Noyce, George Lowe, Michael Westmacott, Charles Wylie and Tenzing Norgay.

An agreement was reached with the Medical Research Council that the physiologist, Griff Pugh, would also join the team. But if Hunt managed to avoid botanists and naturalists, he found the press a different proposition. *The Times* (who had obtained exclusive newspaper rights) insisted on sending a reporter, James Morris, and it was also considered essential that the expedition have a professional film cameraman. The Himalayan Committee had agreed a contract with Countryman Films Ltd, that had helped boost finances. The gentleman selected to make the film was Tom Stobart. Together with the high altitude porters this was the composition of the party.

Hunt's Plan

Colonel John Hunt's plan was structured to allow three attempts on the summit on successive days. On 8 March the expedition assembled at Kathmandu. The first group left the capital on 10 March with 150 porters; the rest followed a day later with a further 200 porters. So the expedition was now split in two and separated by a day's march.

What a sight they must have been as they slowly moved through the rice fields, down the deep valleys, across the rickety bridges spanning the swiftly flowing rivers and up the Magnolia-covered hillsides. It is a big country with great views across to broad expanses of mountainside. Everything throbs with life; it is fertile and dotted with cottages and friendly people. Up and round they went into the rhododendron forests, whose blossoms delight the eye, with colours ranging from scarlet to pink and eventually, above 10,000 feet (3,000 m), to yellow and white. Sherpa and Sahib were united by the hope and the belief that they would succeed.

As the mountain sides became more precipitous and rugged, the scenery at first seemed alpine, only ultimately turning truly Himalayan. The Sherpas zig-zagged up the rocky terrain like an army of leaf-carrying migratory ants, following in the footsteps of all those expeditions that had gone before them. They climbed down to the deep gorge of the Dudgh Kosi river, which is joined by its tributary of Bhote Kosi. On 25 March, they arrived at the colourful Sherpa capital of Namche Bazaar. There the people greeted them with a barrel of milky-coloured 'Chang', a beer brewed from rice. It seems harmless enough, but appearances can be deceptive, and after a few mugs you don't know whether you are in Nepal or Northampton.

By 27 March both halves of the expedition had united at Thyanboche (12,687 feet – 3,806 m), which is dominated by its beautiful Buddhist monastery. This was early in the season but Hunt was determined to allow an acclimatisation period before the start of any serious climbing.

The combination of the two men – Charles Wylie as expedition organiser and Tenzing Norgay as Sirdar worked splendidly.

At Thyanboche there was still a tremendous amount of work to be done, and Hunt and Wylie worked round the clock to make sure that food stocks were plentiful and that every scrap of equipment was in order. Hunt's target was to have the expedition ready to climb the mountain by 15 May before the onset of the monsoon snows when conditions on the mountain would make climbing impossible. They spent the next three weeks, until 20 April, in training and preparing themselves. During this period, Hunt divided them into three parties, one led by Edmund Hillary, one by Charles Evans and the third by Hunt himself. They embarked on treks to greater altitudes and tried out the oxygen equipment. An elite band of Sherpas were instructed in the use of

oxygen. This has not been attempted before, but it was an important part of the plan that six or more of these fine men should be able to climb above the South Col with the summit parties.

These little expeditions were a great success. Morale was high and there was considerable confidence in the oxygen equipment, both in design and effect.

Hunt was determined that the dreaded Khumbu Ice Fall would be given a thorough reconnaissance and a party was composed for this task. It consisted of Edmund Hillary, whose previous knowledge of the Ice Fall would be invaluable; his New Zealand climbing friend, George Lowe, because of his outstanding 'ice-craft'; George Band, who would also be in charge of the wireless equipment and Michael Westmacott, who was to be responsible for the structural equipment, such as ladders that were needed for this section of the route. Griff Pugh and Tom Stobart were added to the party.

On 9 April they set off for the Khumbu Glacier accompanied by five high-altitude Sherpas and 39 porters, many of whom were women. That night they camped at Phalong Karpo and the following night at Lobuje (16,174 feet – 4,852 m). From here they climbed more steeply towards the terminal moraine of the Khumbu Glacier and arrived at Gorak Shep with its tiny green lake below the dark rocky summit of Kala Patter (18,188 feet – 5,456 m) which affords fabulous views of Everest. From here they moved up the tough undulating landscape of the glacier, and on 12 April pitched their tents amongst the great ice pinnacles at the bottom of the Ice Fall at 17,500 feet (5,250 m) – Base Camp was finally established!

On 13 April, Band, Westmacott and Hillary, with four Sherpas carrying tents and food, made a first reconnaissance of the Ice Fall. After five tortuous hours they got within a few hundred yards of where the Swiss had established Camp II the previous year. It had been a terrible struggle. They returned the next day and were appalled to find that fresh blocks of ice had fallen into parts of the route that they had established.

Back at Base Camp that night they received a note from Hunt telling them that he, Ward and Noyce had arrived at Gorak Shep and that they would probably arrive to join them next day.

Hillary's group were determined to greet their leader with the news that they had forced a way through the Ice Fall. So the next day they set out to establish Camp II. Westmacott was ill, so Hillary took Lowe and Band and three Sherpas. This determined but jolly party was joined by physiologist Pugh and cameraman Stobart. Without too much trouble the group arrived at the place where

Camp II was to be established and began to pitch their tents and unload stores. Stobart and Pugh went down with the Sherpas and Hillary and his party camped out on the ice.

I can only say that it is not a place I would have relished spending the night. As they crawled out of their tents the following morning, the difficulties of the Upper Ice Fall looked frightful, but with care they made it through to the brink of the Cwm where they discovered the ideal spot to place Camp III – a safe hollow that gave protection from any avalanche. Hillary was jubilant! They had broken through the hateful Ice Fall. On 22 April, Camp III was established above the Ice Fall at 20,200 feet (6,060 m).

Gorak Shep had served as a lower Base Camp but now all the equipment and supplies were brought up to the Khumbu Glacier Camp. On this momentous day too, the final stores arrived from Kathmandu and the expedition was complete.

Hunt's carefully calculated plan was working perfectly. His approach was like a steady siege, slow and methodical. But it was paying off as a steady stream of Sherpas and climbers successfully began the lift of supplies into the Western Cwm, and then up to the foot of the Lhotse Face.

Camp IV was established at 21,200 feet (6,360 m), Camp V at 22,000 feet (6,600 m) and Camp VI at 23,000 feet (6,900 m) on the face.

The Teams

From the outset Hunt had considered Hillary and Tenzing potentially his strongest pairing, although they had never met before. The first impression these two climbers made on each other makes fascinating reading. Tenzing said:

> Hillary was a wonderful climber – especially on snow and ice, with which he had much practice in New Zealand – and had great strength and endurance. Like many men of action, and especially the British, he did not talk much but he was nevertheless a fine cheerful companion; and he was popular with the Sherpas, because in things like food and equipment he always shared whatever he had. I suppose we made a funny-looking pair, he and I, with Hillary about six feet three inches and myself seven inches shorter. But we were not worrying about that. What was important was that, as we climbed together and became used to each other, we were becoming a strong and confident team.

Left: *The Sherpa capital, Namche Bazaar. This is one of a number of photographs of the journey to Everest taken by* Daily Mail *correspondent Ralph Izzard. Together with Reuters' man Peter Jackson, Izzard followed the expedition through Nepal in an attempt to scoop the* The Times' *exclusive coverage of the ascent.* The Times' *correspondent James Morris would, however, be the one to break the story the first.*

Hillary wrote:

> If you accept the modern philosophy that there must be a ruthless and selfish motivation to succeed in sport, then it could be justly claimed that Tenzing and I were the closest approximation we had on our expedition to the climbing 'prima donnas' of today. We wanted for the expedition to succeed – and nobody worked harder to ensure that it did – but in both our minds success was always equated with us being somewhere around the Summit when it happened.

Another strong pairing was that of Charles Evans and Tom Bourdillon. Bourdillon, in Hunt's words, was built like a second-row rugby forward! He was 28 and had been with Shipton in both the 1951 and 1952.

Charles Evans, besides being deputy leader and climber, was also a doctor but he declined to use the latter distinction, as he felt that he had more than enough responsibilities. Dr Michael Ward, who was a first class climber, was therefore appointed as the official MO. Hunt also instructed him to assist Pugh in his work.

Evans, aged 33, was actually a specialist brain surgeon from Liverpool. He had been to the Himalayas on three occasions, climbing on Cho-Oyu, the Annapurna Massif and to Kulu.

What I am trying to point out is that Tenzing and Hillary were not 'head and shoulders' above the rest. You could form any permutation you liked from the 12 climbers of the expedition and they would all (with luck) stand a reasonable chance of reaching the summit. Wilfred Noyce for instance, aged 34, had reached the summit of Pauhuni (23,400 feet – 7,020 m) in Sikkim. Noyce had been an instructor in mountain warfare in Wales and during the war in Kashmir. In fact, before the war he was known as the 'golden boy' of British climbing – a formidable man. Charles Wylie too, had done considerable climbing in the Garwal Himalaya. George Lowe at 28 was five years younger than his friend Edmund Hillary, yet he had been climbing longer and had introduced Hillary to some of the toughest New Zealand climbs. Lowe was of medium height with a stocky build and was a fine all round climber, with a reputation for great stamina. And what of Henry Cecil John Hunt himself? The gallant leader had climbed in the Alps, when he was only 15 years old. His first ascent was a traverse of Piz Palu. He took part in a marvellous lightweight assault on Saltoro Kangri (25,400 feet – 7,620 m) in the Karakorum, and got within 1,000 feet (300 m) of the top. The Himalayan Committee in London consid-

ered Hunt a 'terrific thruster' even though he was now almost 43 years old.

On 2 May Hunt, Bourdillon and Evans had been reconnoitering the Lhotse Face above Camp V and trying out the closed-circuit oxygen apparatus. The reconnaissance exhausted Hunt and though the apparatus had worked efficiently enough, Evans felt that it was too heavy and had made him feel too hot. Back at Base Camp everyone observed how pale, drawn and tired Hunt looked but he did seem to have amazing powers of recovery. Ward wrote:

> He looked dreadful but this was normal. I wondered how much longer he could go on flogging himself during the day, yet seeming to recover after a night's rest. Almost every time that I had seen him, over the last two weeks, he had looked the same and I had grave doubts about his ability to function efficiently high on the mountain.

Above: *Together with the expedition's official photographer Tom Stobart, the ascent was also recorded by Alfred Gregory. At 39, Gregory was the oldest member of the climbing party.*

Final Plans

The 7th of May 1953 was a very important date. Hunt called a conference in the mess tent at Base Camp to announce his plans for the final assault. It must have been a tense moment for the entire team. After this meeting they would know their roles for the final phase of the expedition. Among the weather-beaten faces in the tent was James Morris of *The Times*, waiting to write down the news and send his next despatch.

For once the climbers mouths were not dry from dehydration. This time, it was from tension and expectancy. Now each man would learn his fate. Would he be chosen to make a summit bid? Hunt, who had been low-key and gentle in his approach until then, now had to lay down the various roles for the team and brook no argument. He knew full well how bitterly disappointed some members would be.

He told them that he had the resources, both in materials and man-power, to mount only one strong attempt on the summit. He emphasised the importance of building up Camp VI (21,200 feet – 6,360 m) into an advanced Base Camp. From this foundation a route could be found up the intimidating Lhotse Face to the South Col, where Camp VIII could then be established. He maintained that his policy was still one of reconnaissance and build-up of supplies and only then, the final thrust upward, not unlike the siege tactics employed by General Bruce in the 1920's expeditions. Hunt still saw the assault as a concentrated military operation. This was the last battle and he was determined to win it.

The difficulties of the Lhotse Face required skilled ice craft and he gave this job to George Lowe, assisted by Westmacott and Band. Once they had solved the mysteries of the face and had fixed the thousands of feet of

Below: *The camp at the Ice Fall. After surmounting this obstacle, the enormous Lhotse Face awaited Hunt's men.*

rope, Wilfred Noyce and Charles Wylie would have the arduous task of getting the Sherpas up the South Col. Pausing for a few seconds for breath, Hunt at last revealed what they were all waiting for, the summit plans in detail.

Weather permitting, there would be two assaults, 24 hours apart. Oxygen would be used from above Camp V (22,000 feet – 6,600 m). The first summit bid would be made from the South Col by Bourdillon and Evans using closed-circuit apparatus. They would make a bid for the South Summit (28,700 feet – 8,610 m) and, if they had enough oxygen and everything was going well, they would press on to the final peak. One day behind would be Hillary and Tenzing, using the open-circuit apparatus with a strong support party of Hunt, Gregory and four or five Sherpas who were to establish a light camp (Camp IX) at about 28,000 feet (8,400m) and then return to the Col.

Dr Mike Ward was not happy about the plan and felt that Hunt should not be leading the team who were to establish Camp IX, "I did not think he would be fit enough and my conclusion was based on his age and performance to date."

Whatever reservations some members of the team might have had, they all settled into their roles and over the next three weeks gave 100 per cent to the enterprise. Before any bid could be made for the summit, the gigantic Lhotse Face had to be dealt with and conquered.

Thus far, Everest had behaved herself, and, apart from the afternoon snow falls, the weather had been surprisingly agreeable. Then her mood changed.

As Lowe and his companions probed the defences of the face, the winds tore at their bodies with merciless intensity. George Band developed a bad cold and had to go down. Mike Westmacott, like Band, had the courage of a lion but he simply could not acclimatise properly for work at high altitude. He felt weak and breathless but continued for a few days to carry loads between Camps V and VI (23,500 feet – 7,050 m) until he was unable to go further. Hunt, who had come up to see what progress they were making, immediately ordered him down. Lowe stuck to his task with the aid of the gallant Sherpas: Da Tenzing, Gyalen, Ang Namgyal and Ang Nyima.

Nyima actually matched Lowe for toughness and stamina. Even so their progress was slow. Hunt observed at the time:

12th May. It is difficult not to feel bitter disappointment in these atrocious weather conditions. Today it has snowed another seven inches [17.5 cm] and this evening I found the track both up and

down the Cwm was obliterated. George Lowe . . . was waist deep at times and his hard-won tracks will have been completely filled in. We've got to solve the Lhotse Face problem and put the best men on to this, regardless of other tasks.

On the 15th Ang Nyima went down for a rest and Wilf Noyce took his place as Lowe's companion. That night Lowe took a sleeping pill for the first time. It had a ghastly effect. The next morning he couldn't wake up. Noyce tried shouting and pummelling him but it was all to no avail and precious time was lost. Eventually, when they did get away it was 10.30 a.m. As they started up the well-worn tracks Lowe kept falling asleep again and they were compelled to return to Camp VI. A whole day had been wasted. But on 17 May, fully recovered and well rested, Lowe at last established Camp VII at 24,000 feet (7,200 m).

They still had over 2,000 feet (600 m) to go, which included a traverse of about 3,000 feet (800 m). Noyce now went down to Camp V, for he was to be responsible, along with Wylie, for supervising the first big carry up to the Col.

Mike Ward was delighted to fill the void left by Westmacott and Band and now replaced Noyce. On 18 May, Ward went up to join Lowe and had huge problems reaching Camp VII. The weather was deteriorating. The following day, after ascending only 200 feet (60 m), fierce cold and icy winds forced Lowe, Ward and Da Tenzing to turn back. They spent the day on 19 May in the tent and barely reached the previous high point on the following day. Things looked bad and there seemed no prospect of progress. The upward drive of the expedition seemed to have come to a halt. Observers down below at Advanced Base Camp were feeling very disappointed and frustrated.

Hunt now decided that Noyce and the Sherpas should go up to Camp VII and try and force their way through to the Col. Noyce went up to Camp VII on 20 May. The next day was the turning point of the expedition.

The threat that the monsoon might arrive early was in everyone's mind. Time was running out. Twelve days had been spent on the Lhotse Face (much longer than Hunt had anticipated) and it still wasn't conquered. Nerves were frayed and the tension was unbearable. Hillary observed from Advanced Base:

We watched eagerly for any sign of action. Finally, two figures, Wilf Noyce and Sherpa Annullu, moved above Camp VII and with immense excitement we watched them climb slowly across

Above: *The Lhotse Face could only be conquered with skilled ice craft. In preparation for the task, during an acclimatisation climb before the ascent of Everest, Charles Evans cuts steps to make a traverse across an almost sheer face of ice.*

the Lhotse Face to the South Col at 26,200 feet (7,860 m). It was a tremendous step forward for the expedition. In a 'backing up' movement on the same day Charles Wylie and another group of Sherpas went from Camp V to Camp VII. This meant that 14 Sherpas (our entire altitude team) were at Camp VII and it was absolutely essential that on the 22nd the whole bunch should go to the South Col or food would run out and the attack would break down.

Because of the mammoth task Wylie had on his hands leading 14 Sherpas up to the Col, Hunt decided, after a great deal of deliberation, to send Hillary and Tenzing up to Camp VII to give fresh impetus to the party. Tenzing, more than anyone, would be able to encourage the Sherpas. Hunt did not reach this decision easily. It is a fact that if you exhaust yourself on Everest, it can take a long period of time to recover, even for titans like Hillary and Tenzing.

With the summit bid now a strong possibility, Hunt was nervous about throwing his crack troops into battle too soon. He need not have worried. They left at 12.15

p.m. on 21 May and arrived at Camp VII after four hours and 15 minutes. The next day, as Noyce and Annulla went down again to Advanced Base for a well-earned rest, Hillary and Tenzing led Wylie and his Sherpas up to the South Col. Hillary describes this ascent vividly:

Tenzing and I were using oxygen, as was Charles Wylie . . . but not the Porters. Tenzing and I went ahead kicking and cutting steps. We made height quite well to the top of the Lhotse Glacier but the Sherpas were going slower and slower . . . some even lying down on the slope and all very tired. Two of them were in considerable distress, so Tenzing and I each took an oxygen bottle from their loads. We continued making the trail and finally breasted the Lhotse ridge. Meanwhile one of the Sherpas had given up and Charles Wylie took from his load a 20lb (8kg) bottle of oxygen. Tenzing and I descended to the desolate windswept South Col and dumped our loads by the wrecks of the Swiss tents. What a place! The South Summit looked absolutely terrific from here. Three of the hardier Sherpas arrived and got rid of their loads and Tenzing and I left the remainder of our oxygen on the Col too. We climbed back up the little slope to the top of the face and met the rest of the Sherpas and Charles Wylie with a solid load. We then plunged down across the traverse picking up the exhausted Sherpa on the way. We ground down to Camp VII and a brief rest and drink . . . then six of us carried on down to Camp IV, passing John Hunt, Tom Bourdillon and Charles Evans at Camp V on their way for the first attempts on the summit.

Hillary and Tenzing were back in Advanced Base Camp. It had been a stupendous performance from this pair. They had gone from Camp IV to Camp VII in one day and from Camp VII to the South Col and back to Camp IV in another. Which meant that they had gone from 21,000 feet to 26,000 feet (6,300-7,800 m) and back in less than 30 hours. Now they would have two days rest before returning for their summit bid.

On 24 May, Bourdillon, Evans, Hunt and the two Sherpas ascended in bad weather conditions and finally arrived at the dreary and desolate South Col. The wind was blowing fiercely and they observed the four skeletons of the Swiss tents from the year before.

I will divert here for a moment, if you will indulge me, as I am eager to tell you about my first 20 minutes on the Col in 1993.

Experiencing the Col

I had enjoyed a rather euphoric ascent of the Lhotse Face. I was a member of the second assault team and unlike Hunt in 1953, I had the benefit of the tents having already been pitched by the previous party. Despite the frightful wind, I embarked on a zany luxurious stroll around the God-forsaken area. Circumnavigating some snow drifts, I came upon the body of one of the four Indian climbers, who had died of exposure on the South Col in 1985. He was sitting upright in the snow, as if he'd just completed morning tea. The cowl on his duvet covered his head and the flesh on his face was drawn tight as a drum and his skin was blue-black in colour. I sat alongside him and whispered a silent prayer. Though his dark goggles were still intact, I could see his sightless eyes peering out in abject misery. What suffering he must have gone through. For he was sitting outside his tent, just seconds away from safety. But after his slow ascent of the Lhotse Face, he had been so weak and his

hands had been so frozen, he had been unable to draw down the zip of his tent. As I looked at him I noticed that his hand was still stuck to the zip, as the remains of the shredded tent fluttered in the wind. Apparently on that night, when he arrived on the Col, there had been climbers from another expedition nearby, all tucked up in their sleeping bags. His howls for help were mistaken for the sound of the wind and he died in despair.

Forgive me for this diversion in the story but I wanted to make you aware of how deadly dangerous the Col can be, and what a thin line there is between success and failure and between tragedy and triumph. So now we return to Hunt and his companions in their tents on the South Col. Though the Swiss had preceded them, the British were still very much a pioneering expedition. Apart from the ever present dangers of the elements and the terrain, there was above all the great psychological barrier of climbing above 28,200 feet (8,460 m), climbing where no man had been before. Could it be done? What would

Above: *One of the photographs taken by Alfred Gregory: Tenzing and Hillary at 27,200 feet (8,160 m), below the crest of the South East Ridge.*

Above: *Camp VIII on the South Col, from which Bourdillon and Evans made their summit attempt on 26 May. The two men were to make it to the mountain's South Summit but no higher. The final goal was within sight, but still out of reach.*

happen to the climbers if they did? It was still a mystery.

On From the Col

The ascent of the South Col had created some difficulties. The closed-circuit apparatus had developed faults and both Evans and Hunt had experienced difficulties with it. As they lay in their tents that night, Bourdillon and Evans must have prayed that the oxygen system would prove reliable and enable them to fulfil their dream of being the very first men to set foot on the summit. In theory the closed-circuit system should give them the speed to get to the top safely but what if it failed or ran out near the summit? The sudden withdrawal of a flow of almost pure oxygen could have disastrous effects.

The next day, 25 May was a rest day. They were all tired after their exertions getting to the Col and they needed to take the time to prepare their gear for the next day's climb.

On the 26th, Ang Tenzing did not feel well and told Hunt that he was not going to move. Hunt was a little annoyed and wrote in his diary that he considered him a 'shirker'! This 'shirking' meant that he and Da Namgyal were forced to share out and carry Ang Tenzing's load.

At 7.00 a.m. they set off for the South East Ridge to establish a light camp at about 28,000 feet (8,400 m) for the second assault team. They were using the open-circuit oxygen system. Evans and Bourdillon, unloaded, free of load carrying, started later at 7.50 a.m. because of problems with their closed-circuit apparatus. They soon caught up with Hunt and Da Namgyal and pressed on until they were out of sight. The weather did not look promising and clouds were gathering up to the East. The heavy loads and increasing steepness of the snow slope were already making Hunt and Da Namgyal dig deep into their reservoir of stamina. Hour after hour they pressed on. Hunt did not realise it at the time but the breathing tube in his oxygen set was choked with ice. And the strain of breathing almost overwhelmed him.

They climbed the Couloir, which rises in steepness to fifty degrees near its top and scrambled to the crest of the South East Ridge at about 27,300 (8,190 m) and came across the ragged remains of Tenzing and Lambert's tent from the previous spring. They now rested for half an hour and then struggled up another 200 feet (60 m). At this point the splendid Da Namgyal signalled that he could continue no further. The weather was now deteriorating rapidly and after making a feeble effort to scrape out a platform, they dumped their loads of food, tents, oxygen and kerosene and started their descent without oxygen.

Meanwhile, Bourdillon and Evans had been making terrific progress. The problems of the closed-circuit oxygen apparatus seemed to have been overcome, though Evans's set could give him only two litres a minute instead of the desired four. Still they were motoring along nicely and they covered the first 1,300 feet (390 m) in an hour and a half. If they could keep up this rate, they would, in all probability, be able to reach the summit by about 12.00 noon.

Everest, however, was not in the mood to co-operate. The clouds intensified and it started to snow. Their pace slowed down and it took two hours to cover the next 700 feet (210 m). They reached 28,250 feet (8,475 m), the high point reached by Tenzing and Lambert the previous year. They crossed the great psychological barrier into the unknown – into territory that had never before felt the footfalls of a human being.

They needed to change the soda-lime canisters in their oxygen sets for fresh ones. The canisters had a life of about 3½ hours. The snow and wind made this a very tricky operation and Evans found that he had great problems breathing at all. After making several adjustments the flow of oxygen returned intermittently, but it was a worrying time for both of them. Even so, they continued the ascent.

The angle steepened and the snow was unstable. On and on they went; every step was agony for Evans. At last the South Summit loomed before them. In the bitterly freezing air, their outer shell clothing was encrusted with white frost and icicles hung from Evans' beard. But on they went and forced their unwilling legs upwards until they reached the South Summit at 28,700 feet (8,610 m)! Now they were higher than any man had been before and they were able to examine the final ridge to the summit of Everest.

In Sight of the Summit

It was an awesome sight: narrow and steep with terrifying drops on either side and great cornices jutting out over the Kangshung Face. It was 1.00 p.m. They had been climbing for 5½ hours and they were exhausted. The question, of course, was whether they could go on. They were well into their second canister of oxygen but the summit was so tantalisingly within their grasp. There was certainly a fair chance that they could reach it but would they return to tell the tale? Would they run out of oxygen near the summit?

Bourdillon was prepared to risk all; Evans was not and his oxygen set was still malfunctioning. They then had the 'highest' argument in the world, which must have looked weird, each man removing his oxygen mask to

Below: *Too exhausted to even take off their kit, Bourdillon and Evans rest at Camp VII after their return from the South Col. The day before, the two men had climbed higher than any other, only to be forced to retreat because of the worsening conditions on the South Summit and problems with their oxygen. Both men were using the closed system.*

make his point. It became quite heated and Bourdillon was all for making a solo effort. He went down in the dip beyond the South Summit and then, perhaps weighing up his chances further, realised that Evans had a point and that they needed to go down. Evans was the elder of the two and Hunt had put him in charge. Frustratingly, retreat was the only course open to them.

It was a nightmare descent and they only just managed to get back, which served to confirm Evans' judgement. Had they pushed on for the summit, they most certainly would have died. They had slipped and tumbled, Evans' oxygen set had continued to malfunction but by some clever tinkering, Boudillon had managed to convert it into an open-circuit system. They had fallen almost out of control down most of the final gully leading to the South Col. It had been a magnificent, noble effort and Hillary's account says it all:

The two men were an awe-inspiring sight! Clad in all their bulky clothes with their great loads of oxygen on their backs and the masks on their faces, they looked like figures from another world. They moved silently towards us – a few stiff, jerky paces – then stop! Then a few more paces! They were very near to complete exhaustion. With a lump in my throat, I climbed up to where they now stood waiting silent with bowed shoulders. From head to foot they were encased in ice. There was ice on their clothing, on their oxygen sets and on their rope. It was hanging from their hair and beards and eyebrows: they must have had the most terrible time in the wind and snow!

Bourdillon and Evans lay exhausted in their tents. Under the tender care of Tenzing and Hillary, they drank about two quarts of liquid.

"Tenzing, I'm confident you and Hillary will do it," said Evans, "but its hard going and will take four or five hours from the High Camp. Its dangerous too – very steep and with cornices – and you must be careful. But if the weather is good you'll do it. You won't have to come back again next year."

John Hunt too, was exhausted after his carry and, while he lay in his tent in his sleeping bag, Tenzing provided him with a supply of lemon-juice and tea.

Though the deeds of these heroic climbers had warmed the hearts of all encamped on the South Col, Everest herself remained cold and indifferent. The night of 26 May was one of the worst on the expedition. The temperature plunged to -25°C and the dreaded sound of the distant 'express trains' heralded the approach of the

Left: The second assault on the summit begins. Edmund Hillary climbs up to the South East Ridge from the South Col on the morning of 28 May. The party sent to establish the final camp on 28 May consisted of two groups. George Lowe, Arthur Gregory and Sherpa Ang Nyima went first, while Hillary and Tenzing followed about an hour afterwards.

fiendish west wind. With depressing power it battered the tents, pouring scorn on the mens' achievements.

Tenzing, Lowe, Gregory and Hillary were in the Pyramid Tent. Hunt, Bourdillon and Evans crammed in the Meade and there were three Sherpas in the small Dome. All were breathing a little night oxygen. With the wind so appalling and the temperature so low, it must have crossed all their minds that this was possibly the end of the expedition. There was no respite in the morning and it was impossible to get warm. Throughout the night Evans and Bourdillon had shown signs of deterioration, Bourdillon alarmingly so. It was imperative that they should descend as quickly as possible, in spite of the bad weather. Ang Temba had also been sick all night and so he was to go down as well.

Bourdillon's Collapse

Scarcely had the three left the tents, when Bourdillon collapsed in the snow. He was given oxygen and liquid which revived the big man but shortly after this, he collapsed again. He was now in danger of losing his life and someone would have to go down with him if he was to reach safety. Hunt's plan was that Hillary and Tenzing's assault would be supported by Gregory and two Sherpas. The fact that Lowe had turned up was an added bonus, yet, strictly speaking, both he and Hunt were not needed. There was nothing that Hunt could do except sit and wait at the South Col. He had already been very high and had been three days at the Col. A tremendous performance certainly but one that had weakened him considerably.

Of the two men, Lowe, now much rested, would be of much more help to Gregory's support team than Hunt. But oh! Hunt could not bear not being involved in the action and rank did have its privileges. He ordered Lowe to go down with Bourdillon. Lowe was flabbergasted and protested vehemently against it, supported passionately by his good friend Hillary. It was all to no avail; he was to go down as ordered. It wasn't until Lowe was about to go, that Hunt suddenly changed his mind and said that he would go down instead. Hillary wrote: "I have never admired him more than for this difficult decision."

In the spring of 1990 I had the good fortune to meet Lord Hunt (as he is now titled) and I questioned him about his decision to descend with Bourdillon. He paused for a while, then flashed me a charming smile and said, "I was the leader but more importantly I was a member of the first assault team. My duty was to see them safely down the mountain."

So on 27 May Hunt went down with Evans, Bourdillon and Ang Temba. Hillary grimly remarked: "It was the blind leading the blind." They set off and, after a difficult descent, reached Camp VII, where Mike Ward was resident.

There were now six people at the Col – Lowe, Gregory, Hillary, Ang Nyima, Pemba and Tenzing. Hours dragged by and they lay in their tents shivering, drinking great quantities of liquid and listening to the sound of the wind against the canvas of the tent. Night came and the weather was still bad.

As Tenzing lay in the darkness listening to the wind he thought:

It must stop, so that tomorrow we can go up. I have been seven times to Everest. I love Everest but seven times is enough. It must be now. So

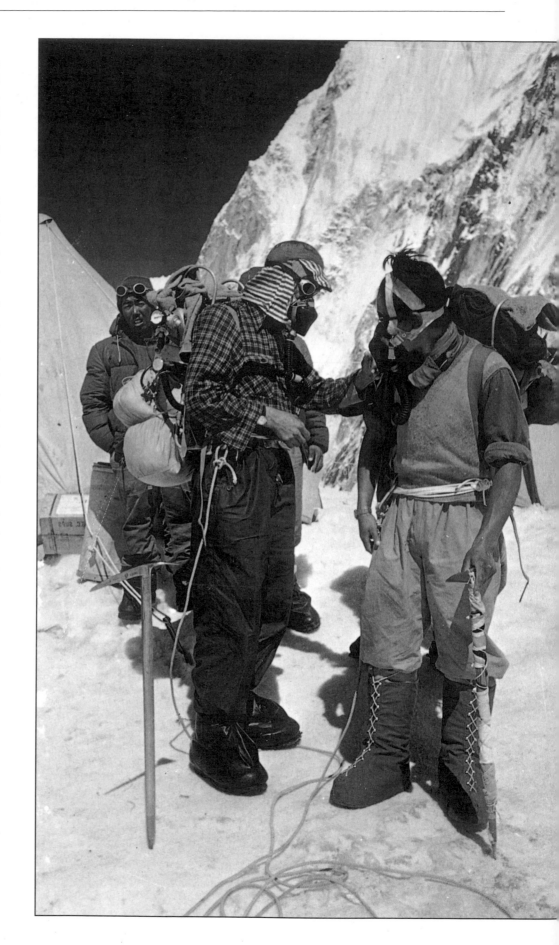

Above and left: *The climb started at 8.45 a.m. and finished at 2.30 p.m. After some anxious moments searching for a suitable site, the final camp was established at 27,900 feet (8,370 m). Lowe, Gregory and Ang Nyima dumped over 125 lbs (50 kg) of equipment with Hillary and Tenzing and headed back down the mountain. The two men were now on their own to cope with the night's freezing temperatures as best they could, and prepare for the summit attempt the following day – 29 May.*

many men have died on Everest, like a battlefield but some day a man must win.

The 28th of May was fine and windy. Unfortunately, Pemba was ill, leaving only one Sherpa. The presence of George Lowe was now much appreciated. The objective was to pitch a final camp as high as possible. All previous expeditions had failed because the highest camp had always proved to be too low, leaving the climbers too much to do on the final day. Mallory had emphasised the importance of this high camp as early as 1922. Now in 1953 Hillary and company were determined to solve this problem.

To the Final Camp

The support team moved off first, at 8.45 a.m., Lowe in the lead carrying 45 lbs (18 kg) of stores, Gregory with 40 lbs (16 kg) each. Hillary and Tenzing followed at 10.00 a.m. and though they were supposed to conserve their energy, carried two oxygen bottles each, plus all their personal and camping gear, cameras, food, etc. . . at least 50 lbs (20 kg). The luxury they enjoyed was being able to follow the tracks Lowe and Company were making clear ahead of them. They were all using the open-circuit apparatus.

The two groups came together at the battered remains of the Swiss tent at 27,200 feet (8,160 m) and from there on climbed together. After another 150 feet (45 m) they came across the dump made by Hunt and Da Namgyal of a tent, fuel, food and oxygen. After some discussion, they decided to push on still further carrying all the gear. Hillary took on the tent, which made his load over 60 lbs

(18 kg) and the others divided the rest. They moved up the Ridge with Lowe leading the way. With backs bent and breathing laboured, they pressed on upwards in a determined bid to establish the desired High Camp but they could not find a suitable spot. The ridge grew steeper and their pace was now very slow. By 2.00 p.m. they were nearing exhaustion and it was agreed that it was urgent to find a suitable camping site.

The position was getting desperate, when Tenzing took the lead over deep unstable snow in search of a place he had spotted the year before with Lambert.

Finally they got there, a flatish spot in the shelter of a rocky bluff. They dropped their loads and with a quick "Good-bye" and "Good Luck", Lowe, Gregory and Ang Nyima started back to the South Col. It was 2.30 p.m. and they were at 27,900 feet (8,370 m). A new world record. They had established the highest camp in Everest's history. At last, two men were at the right height at the right time.

The first task was to try and make the spot more suitable for erecting a tent. Both Hillary and Tenzing were in superb condition and found that they could chop out the ice and erect the tent without using oxygen. They had no effective means of tying down the tent, so they hitched ropes to corners of rocks and to oxygen bottles anchored deep in the snow and prayed for good weather!

The Last Night

At 6.00 p.m. they moved into the tent. That evening they dined well on soup, sardines on biscuits, a tin of apricots, dates and biscuits with jam. Tenzing recorded that 'like camels' they drank large amounts of very sweet lemon water and coffee.

The thermometer registered -27°C, yet they did not feel unduly cold, as the wind was generally steady with only the occasional strong gusts.

Hillary made an inventory of the oxygen supplies and found that they had only 1¾ cylinders each for the assault. He calculated that they could make an attack using about three litres a minute, if they relied on finding the two, one-third full bottles left by Bourdillon and Evans at about 500 feet (150 m) below the summit. They had little oxygen to spare for sleeping and Hillary decided to use it at one litre a minute in two shifts: from 9.00 p.m. to 11.00 p.m., and from 1.00 a.m. to 3.00 a.m. Lying in the dark they talked of their plans for the next day. There they were, all alone at 27,900 feet (8,370 m) on the highest mountain on planet Earth. Yet, in a way they were not alone. For news had already filtered throughout the world that the British expedition was high on Everest and about to make a final assault.

Below: *This was the route that faced Hillary and Tenzing, the final part of the South East Ridge leading to the summit. The obstacle now known as the Hillary Step can be seen half way up. The problems faced are the same today as they were then. When climbing the route, great care has to be taken to tread clear of the snow cornices which overhang the face — and a sheer drop.*

Summit Attempt

On the morning of 29 May 1953, they awoke at 4.00 a.m. It was a bright, clear dawn and the wind had almost vanished. Tenzing pointed out to Hillary the tiny dot that was the Thyangboche Monastery, 16,000 feet (4,800 m) below. Hillary's boots had been lying outside his sleeping bag all night and had frozen solid. They had to be thawed out over the primus stove. It took 2½ hours to get ready for their bid for the summit as they had to melt snow for drinks and had to fiddle with the oxygen sets.

At 6.30 a.m. they moved off. Hillary's boots were still stiff and his feet cold, so he asked Tenzing to take the lead for a while. They climbed up the ridge, which narrowed considerably, and the crusted snow broke beneath their boots causing them to sink up to their knees at every step. Occasionally they found the footprints of Bourdillon and Evans and were able to use them but mostly they had been wiped away by the winds.

Hillary's feet were now feeling better so they changed places on the rope and kept doing this from then on. They arrived at the snow shoulder, where Evans and Bourdillon had changed oxygen cylinders. Hillary was greatly relieved to discover that the abandoned cylinders were indeed, about one-third full, which meant about an hours supply and a possible life-saver for the descent to the Col.

The narrow ridge led up to the very steep snow face that runs up to the South Summit. From this point Bourdillon had traversed left to reach the rock ridge and he and Evans had moved up from ledge to ledge on unstable rock. Their tracks were faintly visible but both Hillary and Tenzing disliked the route. After a short discussion, they decided to approach the South Summit

'head on' up an almost vertical white wall of snow and ice. As they moved up, they found the conditions very difficult and dangerous. The powdery snow was not firm and kept sliding down, carrying them with it! Being soft there was precious little belay for the ice axe. Tenzing later recalled:

It was one of the most dangerous places I have ever been on a mountain. Even now, when I think of it, I feel as I felt then and the hair almost stands up on the back of my neck.

Hillary shared his feelings:

My solar plexus was tight with fear. It was altogether most unsatisfactory and whenever I felt feelings of fear regarding it, I would say to myself 'Forget it. This is Everest and you have got to take a few risks'.

They both realised that if either of them slipped, there was little chance of arresting the fall and there was also a big risk of starting an avalanche.

They went on and, after several hundred feet, the angle eased off and they were able to belay themselves more safely on various small outcrops of rock.

At last, they cramponed up the firmer snow of the final cone and stood on the top of the South Summit. It was only 9.00 a.m!

When Bourdillon and Evans had reached this point, they had experienced dreadful weather conditions with a howling westerly wind tearing at their bodies and blowing thick snow across the final ridge to the summit. Now the weather was perfect. Small white clouds clung to the valleys below but the sky above them was that intense bright azure blue of high altitude. Most astonishing of all there was hardly a breath of wind. Was Everest perhaps 'in the mood'?

The view was magnificent. In the foreground, surrounded by numerous peaks was mighty Makalu with its great ridges stretching out for miles pointing the way to distant majestic Cho-Oyu, the eighth highest peak in the world. Hillary and Tenzing's great effort had now taken them to 28,700 feet (8,610 m) and, much to their delight, they could now look down on Everest's close neighbour Lhotse, at 27,890 feet (8,367 m).

They had a short rest and Hillary changed both his and Tenzing's oxygen bottles for full ones. With hope in their hearts they looked up at the remaining 300 feet (90 m). The sight ahead was impressive but not disheartening. The ridge was narrower and steeper than it had

been below and, though not impossible, would certainly not be easy. On the left, as before, the precipice fell away to the Western Cwm 8,000 feet (2,400 m) below and on the right, great cornices hung over the terrifying 10,000 foot (3,000 m) abyss of the Kangshung Face. If they were to get to the top, it would be along a narrow line between the precipice and cornices – never too far to the left and never too far to the right or they would plunge to their deaths.

Now that they had discarded the two oxygen bottles, the weight on their backs was reduced from 40 lbs to 20 lbs (12-6 kg). As they left the South Summit, they were also delighted to find the snow was firm and sound.

After descending down a little, after the South Summit, they began to climb steadily upwards again. They moved one at a time, taking turns at going ahead. Progress fell into a steady rhythm. While the leader went ahead, the second man wrapped the rope round his axe and fixed the axe in the snow to act as an anchor. Some of the cornice bumps proved difficult and unstable but they solved this by moving right down onto the rocks on the left and scrambling.

The weather was still fine but they had trouble breathing and had to stop and clear away the ice that kept forming in the pipes of their oxygen sets. After each short stop

Above: *Just one of the views on the way to the summit. Sunrise on Lhotse, seen from 27,500 feet (8,250 m) on the South East Ridge.*

Left: *It is 11.30 a.m., 29 May, 1953, and Tenzing Norgay stands on the summit of Everest. The dream had been accomplished at last. For Tenzing the success held a special significance. After 20 years and six attempts to climb the mountain, he had finally achieved his ambition. The Swiss expedition in 1952 had left him exhausted and hospitalised, but barely a year later his indomitable spirit had taken him back and sent him to the very top. After staying on the summit for 15 minutes Hillary and Tenzing began their descent. They stayed on the South Col that night, and returned to Camp IV the following day. From there the news was to spread around the world.*

they pushed on, twisting and turning and gaining height along the ridge between the cornices and the precipice.

Over the 'Hillary Step'

After an hour or so they came to a vertical rock step in the ridge, about 40 feet (12 m) high and now known as the 'Hillary Step'. Hillary saw a possible way up on the right hand side. A huge snow cornice clung onto the rock step and between the rock and the cornice, a gap had formed because some of the snow had melted. He decided it was just wide enough for a man to get his body into. Tenzing took a secure belay and the tall New Zealander gently eased himself into the gap. Slowly and carefully he pressed backward with his feet against the cornice. The question uppermost in Hillary's mind was, would the pushing of his cramponed boots be enough to send the cornice flying off down the 10,000 foot (3,000 m) Kangshung Face with him on it? Fortunately, the large cornice remained firm.

Gasping for breath and with nerves stretched to the limit, he twisted, squirmed and clawed his way up until he arrived safely at the top. After taking several minutes to get his breath back, he anchored himself firmly and protected Tenzing, as he climbed up the intimidating fissure.

Beyond the 'Hillary Step' the angle of the ridge eased up, though it was still dangerous. The going was much easier and the two men felt now that they were going to reach the summit and that nothing would stop them. They continued with barely suppressed excitement, cutting steps and climbing over the rising undulations. Now the two climbers could move together. They saw a tiny ridge that rose up to a snowy dome. Hillary moved onto it and calmly and slowly cut steps, once more supported on a tight rope by Tenzing. Seconds later, Tenzing was alongside him. Then time stood still, and they moved, as in a dream, up the last few feet of the snow dome.

Climbed at Last

At 11.30 a.m. on 29 May 1953, Tenzing Norgay and Edmund Hillary stepped onto the summit of Mount Everest and became the first men ever to reach the highest point on Earth. This is how Hillary described their historical moment of triumph:

My first sensation was one of relief – relief that the long grind was over; that the summit had been reached before our oxygen supplies had dropped to a critical level; and relief that in the end the mountain had been kind to us in having a pleasantly rounded cone for its summit instead of a fearsome and unapproachable cornice. But mixed with relief was a vague sense of astonishment that I should have been the lucky one to attain the ambition of many brave and determined climbers. It seemed difficult at first to grasp that we'd got there. I was too tired and too conscious of the long way down to safety really to feel any great elation. But as the fact of our success thrust itself more clearly into my mind, I felt a quiet glow of satisfaction spread through my body – a satisfaction less vociferous but more powerful than any I had ever felt on a mountain before. I turned and looked at Tenzing. Even beneath his oxygen mask and the icicles hanging from his hair, I could see his infectious grin of sheer delight. I held out my hand and, in silence, we shook hands in good Anglo-Saxon fashion. But this was not enough for Tenzing and impulsively he threw his arm around my shoulders and we thumped each other on the back in mutual congratulations.

Hillary's thoughts now turned to Mallory and Irvine and the 1924 Expedition and he searched around the summit to see if there were any traces of them but there were none. Later on Hillary said, "Wouldn't Mallory have been pleased?"

He now busied himself taking photographs of Tenzing and the great Sherpa motioned to Hillary that he would like to photograph him. Hillary declined the offer and continued taking shots of the astounding scenery. Tenzing unwound four flags from around his ice-axe, which had been tied together on a string, and stood on the summit for the now famous picture. The flags, from top to bottom, were the United Nations, British, Nepalese and Indian flags. Tenzing was delighted that the United Nations flag was on top, for he liked to think that the victory was for all men everywhere. He then took from his pocket the pack of sweets that he had been carrying and the little red and blue pencil his daughter, Nima, had given him. Scraping a hollow in the snow he laid them in it. Hillary then placed a small black cloth cat, with white eyes, that Hunt had given him as a mascot in the hollow and a crucifix, that the leader had asked to be placed on the summit.

As they covered up the offerings Tenzing said a silent prayer and gave thanks. "Seven times I have come to the mountain of my dream," he whispered, "and on this, the seventh, with God's help, the dream has come true. Thuji chey Chomolungma, I am grateful."

They now spread the flags across the summit and buried the ends of the string firmly in the snow. A few days later planes of the Indian Air Force flew round the peak taking photographs, but the pilots reported that they could see nothing.

Before starting the descent, Hillary and Tenzing had one more look for Mallory and Irvine. There was no sign of them. Yet they simply couldn't get them out of their minds, as they stared down in the direction of Tibet and the familiar landmarks left by earlier expeditions – the Rongbuk Monastery, the Rongbuk and East Rongbuk Glaciers, the North Col and the place near the North East Ridge, where Tenzing had been in 1938, when the British established Camp VI. In the distance, stretching for hundreds of miles, they viewed in wonder the beige and brown carpet of the Tibetan Plateau.

The Descent

They had been on the summit 15 minutes and, after eating some Kendal Mint Cake, they set off again. In an hour they were back at the South Summit. They were anxious to get down as quickly as possible but they knew that they were more tired now and that their reactions were less sure. They therefore needed to exert maximum concentration to avoid an accident. They managed the descent of the dangerous snow face below the South Summit and eventually arrived back at their camp of the previous night. Here Tenzing prepared a lemon drink, while Hillary changed the oxygen cylinders. They had climbed throughout the day on a flow rate of three litres per minute.

At 3.00 p.m., with the oxygen cylinders in place and feeling much refreshed by the warm drinks, they set off again on the last stage of the descent.

The rest of the descent went well and they arrived safely at the bottom of the final couloir and slowly made their way to the camp on the South Col. There to greet them was George Lowe. Hillary waved his ice-axe and shouted out the famous words: "Well George, we knocked the bastard off."

Lowe threw his arms around them and with the help of Noyce, who had come up with Sherpa Pasang Puta, gave them coffee and tea and helped them into the tent.

Down below at Camp IV at 21,000 feet (6,300 m), the whole team was gathered, awaiting news of Hillary and Tenzing's attempt. Their frustrations must have been unbearable, for there was no radio contact with the South Col and a visual signal, which Hunt had arranged, was obscured by thick mists. James Morris, *The Times* correspondent, had put up a tremendous performance by ascending from Base Camp to Camp IV. If the climbers reached the summit, he knew that he would have a staggering scoop on his hands. Stobart was also there with his

trusty camera to film it all for posterity. All was in readiness and yet there was still no sign of the climbers. All eyes were riveted on the Lhotse Face and, after what seemed like a lifetime, they perceived five tiny dots descending. But it still took many hours for the climbers to make their way through the complexities of the Lhotse Glacier. Finally a great shout went up, "There they are!" Everyone surged forward, slipping and slithering over the soft snow in eager anticipation. It didn't look good, for Hillary, Lowe, Tenzing, Noyce and Puta dragged their heels and approached looking very tired and giving no sign of success. They were under orders from Stobart, who had sent a runner up to tell them that if they had good news to hold it back as long as possible, so that he could film the great moment. Hunt, fearing the worst, moved up slowly with his back bent in depressed disappointment. Then suddenly George

Below: *Hillary and Tenzing on their return to Camp IV. Most of the expedition had climbed up to meet them including The Times' correspondent James Morris. The waiting must have been unbearable. Without any radio or visual signal between the camp and the South Col the men at Camp IV had to wait until the assault party were within shouting distance before they found out their expedition had been a magnificent success.*

Lowe, leading the party, raised his arm and waved, at the same time he gave the thumbs up!

Everest was climbed! Hillary held his ice-axe high in weary triumph and Tenzing slipped on his backside and flashed his smile. For a moment Hunt was transfixed. Then, his body rigid with excitement, he ran forward and threw his arms around Hillary and held him close in an embrace of pure gratitude and love. Then he held Tenzing in the same embrace and smacked his back over and over in appreciation. All the members of the expedition shook hands and embraced them. Everyone was smiling, laughing, embracing, taking photographs, smiling again, laughing again and crying.

Releasing the News

As soon as Hillary and Tenzing had eaten an omelette each and given an account of their ascent, James Morris

Below: *Tenzing and Hillary at Camp IV. Soon they were to be the most famous men in the world.*

set off for Base Camp guided by Mike Westmacott, to impart his precious news to Britain. He had to be very careful for rival newspapers such as *The Daily Mail, The Daily Telegraph* and Reuters itself were camped in the Khumbu Valley, waiting like vultures and ready to pick up any tit-bit they could find. Morris was determined to get his message to London in time for the Coronation. Absolute secrecy was essential. He sent a runner to the Indian Police radio post at Namche Bazaar with a coded message: "Snow conditions bad. Stop. Advanced Base abandoned yesterday. Stop. Awaiting improvement. Stop." Decoded this meant: "Summit of Everest reached on 29 May by Hillary and Tenzing. All is well."

The ruse worked perfectly and the British Embassy in Kathmandu transmitted the message on the diplomatic radio to *The Times* headquarters in Queen Victoria Square, London. The Queen was given the message in one of the red despatch boxes and an exclusive despatch appeared in *The Times* on the morning of 2 June, Coronation Day. The newspapers were full of it.

Back on the mountain, the expedition members celebrated the ascent with a plentiful supply of rum. They drank, ate and rested. They toasted everyone who had been part of the history of Everest, in particular Eric Shipton who was no doubt celebrating with them, and Mallory and Irvine were also very much in their thoughts.

That night Camp IV was the centre of the universe. Hunt made an emotional speech of thanks to his team before retiring to his tent. The tremendous strain of leadership for months on end caught up with him and he crawled into the security of his 'cocoon-like' sleeping bag.

James Morris called the expedition, 'the last innocent adventure'. Back in Britain, we celebrated the coronation of a young Queen and rejoiced in the news from the Himalayas. It was a great moment in the history of mountaineering.

Out of interest, during my interview with Lord Hunt in 1990, I asked him what he would have done had Hillary and Tenzing failed to reach the summit? After about 30 seconds he replied: "Possibly I would have mounted a third assault by Wilfred Noyce and myself."

On Wednesday 6 May 1993, at the Royal Geographical Society, Kensington Gore, London, I was lucky enough to attend the 40th anniversary of the first ascent of Everest. As the lights came up, six members of the original expedition – Hillary, Hunt, Band, Wylie, Ward and Pugh – rose from their chairs on the podium to receive the most full-blooded standing ovation I have ever heard. We all recognised that something real and

Right: *Hillary toasts victory – the mug is cameraman Tom Stobart's.*

tangible had taken place in those spring days of 1953 on Everest, and yet despite our joy and acknowledgment of their achievement there was sadness too. Time had passed so quickly. Where had the years gone?

The six glorious men on the platform had white hair and their muscles were rather less supple than they used to be. Four members of the team had died, two of them in mountain accidents. Looking back, John Hunt wrote of the ascent:

Was it worthwhile? For us who took part in the adventure, it was so beyond doubt. We shared a high endeavour; we witnessed scenes of beauty and grandeur; we built up a lasting comradeship among ourselves and we have seen the fruits of that comradeship ripen into achievement. We shall not forget those moments of great living up on that mountain.

The members of the expedition are now variously in the Arts, Medicine, Business, Education and Science. One has become an Ambassador, one the head of a university college and one a peer of the realm.

Hillary has become a legend in Nepal, not just because he climbed Everest but also because of his commitment and dedication to the welfare of the Sherpa people in the Sola Khumbu.

The list of his achievements is endless and includes building schools at Thyanboche, Thami, Namche Bazaar and Chaunrikarka. He has helped construct an airfield at Lukla and a variety of bridges. In this work, he has been helped by his friend, George Lowe, his relatives and many good friends. In 1966, he achieved one of his greatest ambitions and built a hospital for the Sherpas at Kunde at 12,700 feet (3,810 m).

Sadly, Tenzing Norgay is no longer with us. He passed away peacefully at his home in Darjeeling at the age of 67. Like Hillary, he is a legendary figure throughout the world. If I could give him a title then it would be 'The Man Of Everest'. He was the first humbly born Asian climber to attain world stature and fame. Being a simple man with simple tastes, he sometimes found the pressure of fame hard to bear. So much so, that at one time he collapsed and became seriously ill. When the crowds became too big and the greedy and sycophantic homed in on him, his eyes would take on the look of a hunted tiger. It is said that there was a pure flame in Tenzing that was lit by his gentleness and humility and it was these fine qualities that helped him cope in difficult circumstances. One of his proudest achievements was to establish the Himalayan Institute of Mountaineering in Darjeeling. This school was formed to train Sherpas to the high standards of Swiss guides. To attain these standards the Sherpas attended courses set up by the Swiss Foundation.

In the spring of 1990 I met Tenzing's nephew, Gombu, for a coffee outside the old 'Tea Planters Club' in Darjeeling, where the Everestiers had stayed. We were filming a sequence for the film 'Galahad Of Everest'. Since working with the 1953 expedition Gombu has climbed Everest twice, first with the Americans in 1963 and then with the Indian expedition in 1965. Both ascents were by the South East Ridge. He is now the President of the Mountaineering School. I found him a kind, thoughtful character, who laughed frequently, rather like his Uncle Tenzing. He found me 'a hoot' and was much amused by my many questions.

Later he led me up a winding pathway to his climbing museum. Inside a quiet shady room was a modest shrine in which stood a simple earthenware pot. Gombu whispered to me with tears in his eyes, "The ashes of Tenzing."

When I think of that moment with Gombu in that quiet room, I ask myself, what is it really all about? What does it mean to conquer this or that! Conquer what? Tenzing is dead! His ashes are in Darjeeling and yet Everest is as cold, hot, windy and as big as ever. Except for growing a little higher, it hasn't changed noticeably. These so called 'conquests' have had no effect on her at all.

The Head Lama from the Rongbuk Monastery said these wise words to me, as he stuffed his face with Stilton cheese and biscuits from our Fortnum and Masons' food hamper at Base Camp in 1990: "We do not think of conquest. If we, the monks could climb Everest, we would not say we have conquered it."

I suppose at this point in the book it is as good a time as any to ask, what makes Everest so special? The answer,

I presume, is quite simple. Everest has one attribute shared by no other mountain – it is the highest peak in the world. Yet, when I met the Dalai Lama in 1990 he said:

Chomolungma is a very sacred mountain. It is the guardian for Tibetan Buddhist teaching. Besides its height and beauty, I consider it very important. In Tibetan we call it 'Yankiamuntakin'. The top of the mountain appears to touch the blue sky. The name 'Yankiamun' means 'The Majesty, The Queen of Snow Mountain'. 'Takin' means 'blue' or 'dark blue'. So 'Yankiamuntakin' means 'The Queen of the Blue Snow Mountain in the Sky'. The area around Everest, Gyachung Kang and Makalu are the 'power places' that emanate the life

Below: *On 3 July, members of the team flew to London to be fêted and honored. Hunt and Hillary were to be knighted, while Tenzing received the George Medal.*

force. That is why certain mystics spend their entire lives in meditation there.

Climbed But Never Conquered

Many people felt that once Everest was climbed, the magic of the place would be tarnished, forever. The unattainable was attained and that was the end of it. I cannot accept this. There is more to a mountain than getting to the summit! You will see what I mean for yourselves shortly when we climb Everest together. George Leigh Mallory described these feelings perfectly:

A great mountain is always greater than we know; it has mysteries, surprises, hidden purposes, it holds something in store for all of us. It has greatness beyond our guessing – genius if you like – that indefinable something, to which we know but one response: the spirit of adventure.

Within a few years, after Hillary and Tenzing's ascent of Everest, all the major peaks in the mountains of Asia had been climbed: K2 in 1954, Cho-Oyu in 1954, Makalu and Kangchenjunga in 1955, Lhotse, Mustagh Ata and Tomur in 1956, Broad Peak in 1957 and Dhaulagiri in 1960. Incidentally, Charles Evans led the Kangchenjunga expedition, the third highest mountain in the world and reached the summit with George Band and Joe Brown, the Manchester plumber, who was to become a star in his own right. It was a particularly marvellous performance by George Band, for he had suffered badly from altitude sickness on Everest. John Hunt wrote in his diary on 30 May 1953, "Thus ends the epic of Mount Everest.".

In actual fact, this statement couldn't have been further from the truth. Once a breakthrough has been made, be it the four minute mile or swimming the Channel, then the barrier of doubt is down. Other ambitious individuals can be sure that what has been achieved can be repeated and improved on by themselves. Everest was like a magnet and the flood gates opened up.

Previous pages:
Chomolungma's great North Face.

Below: *Sherpanis load-carrying to Everest Base Camp.*

For the next 40 years after 1953, Everest was climbed by the Swiss, Chinese, Indians, Americans, Tibetans, Japanese, Sikkimese, Nepalese, Italian, English, Scots, Irish, Austrians, Germans, French, Poles, Slovenians, Croatians, Spanish Basques, Soviet Russians, Soviet Ukranians, Soviet Kazakh, Canadians, Bulgarians, Australians, Dutch, Slovaks, Norwegians, South Koreans, Spanish Galicians, Spanish Catalan, Macedonians, Mexicans, Belgians, Czechs, Swedes, Spanish Valencian, Spanish Aragonese, Soviet Georgians, Israelis, Hong Kong Chinese, New Zealands, Chileans, Spanish Castilians, Spanish Madrilians, Luxembourgians, Peruvians, Welsh, New Zealand Maoris and Venezuelans.

For individual ascents, Nepali climbers stand at the top of the list with 129. US climbers are second with 68, Japanese third with 35. The full tally of the remaining nationalities (listed according to 1994 boundaries) is: France 26; Spain 25; China 23; India and Russia 20; United Kingdom 17; Italy 14; South Korea 13; New Zealand 11; Switzerland 9; Austria, Poland, Kazakhstan, Australia and Slovenia, 7; Canada and Norway, 6; Bulgaria 5; Netherlands and Chile, 4; Slovakia, Ukraine, Sweden and Mexico, 3; Belgium and Croatia, 2; Macedonia, Georgia, Czech Republic, Israel, Hong Kong, Luxembourg, Peru, and Venuzeula, 1.

Since the summit has been reached, some mountaineers have attempted to put the difficulty back into ascents (if any more were needed) by choosing the harder routes. Others have decided to challenge the mountain by climbing without oxygen.

Since Reinhold Messner's pioneering climb in 1978, over 50 people have reached the summit without oxygen, including the Nepalese Sherpa Ang Rita, who between 1983 and 1992 reached the summit no less than seven times!

All successful ascents are balanced by about a 64 per cent failure rate and, of course, the saga continues, with more and more expeditions planned for the future. Good luck to them, I say, and long may they flourish!

Below: *The mountains and people of the Himalayas are bound together by religion and faith. Tibetan prayer flags frame Shishapangma in the background.*

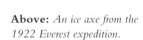

> *'Above the glacier Everest rises not so much a peak as a prodigious mountain mass. There is no complication for the eye. The highest of the world's great mountains, has to make but a simple gesture of magnificence to be lord of all'.*
>
> GEORGE LEIGH MALLORY, 1921[4]

PREPARING FOR OUR CLIMB

THE IDEA OF WRITING this book came about during the British tour of my One Man Show – 'From Childhood to Everest'. The venues had been varied and ranged from concert halls, barns, theatres, village halls and wild rowdy pubs. It was a tremendous experience and I loved every minute of it, though, I must confess, on one occasion I was absolutely petrified when I was asked to give an abridged version at The Royal Geographical Society in London.

I need not have worried, for the kind gathering of renowned explorers gave me a rousing ovation and I was 'tickled pink'. Up and down the country the reaction was the same and audiences everywhere enthusiastically urged me to put down on paper my bizarre obsession for the great mountain. An actor on Everest? Why? The question intrigued them. Even to this day, I can't answer that one. The show seemed to inspire the audiences natural love for adventure. It was obvious that it was a passion that had been bottled up in them since childhood. The mountain became a symbol. "There are Everests everywhere," I said. "In all walks of life." "Yes," replied a woman in Leeds. "I'm going to ride my daughter's horse before I die; I've always been frightened of it." The lady in question by the way, had cancer. "I'm not going to die just because I'm dying," she said.

The tide of people's emotion swept me along from venue to venue and they constantly bombarded me with questions on how they could obtain information on treks

Above: *An ice axe from the 1922 Everest expedition.*

Left: *Jinette Harrison approaches the summit at 28,700 feet (8,610 m). Lhotse is in the background to the left of the climber. Harrison's ascent in October 1993 was only the second ascent by a British woman. The first was made by Rebecca Stephens who made the summit earlier the same year. Her climb coincided with the 40th anniversary of Hunt's expedition.*

Right: *Approaching the summit from the North Face. This will be the final objective of our own climb. The mountaineer here is approaching the Second Step at 28,000 feet (8,400 m). The summit pyramid rises up in the background.*

and expeditions. It was heady stuff and totally new to me. What was refreshing about these shows was the fact that I could be myself – not Brian Blessed the actor, playing a part. I found the experience liberating. Without the use of props, I simply stood there and told the story. At the end of each evening, people felt that they had climbed Everest with me. "Please write a simple book telling these stories, Mr Blessed," many said. "We didn't realise that Everest is so big and that it is still young and growing. It should be a book that young and old alike could read and feel as if they were climbing the mountain with you." It was these simple requests that spurred me on to write this book.

A Few Facts

Before we finally embark on our expedition, allow me to clarify some facts about myself.

From this book you may be under the impression that I am a gifted mountaineer. Nothing could be further from the truth. When asked how I compare to Chris Bonington, Doug Scott or even Messner, my answer is quite simple – "I don't!" You may also think that I am quite a brave chap. This is just not true. "Oh! Sir Brian – as bold as a lion," the poem says. Not so. At the time of writing I am about to start rehearsals for a tour of *The Wizard Of Oz*. You've guessed it. I'm playing The Cowardly Lion, a part much more in keeping with my character. It would be fair to say that, in all my years of climbing at high altitude, I have never come across any mountaineer who is less talented than I. Ah, poor Brian! I can hear you say and I much appreciate the sympathy. My right foot is slightly deformed and points to three o'clock and can give me problems, particularly when descending.

Physically, being large boned and heavily muscled, I am much more suited to judo than mountaineering. Climbers are generally slim individuals, though you do sometimes see the occasional stocky lad or lass. So don't be put off if you are heavy. When Peter Habeler climbed Everest with Messner he said: "What the doubting physiologist fail to recognise was the mysterious 'X Factor' everyone possesses."

That thought has frequently kept me going on a mountain. Heavy lad I may be, but I have always had plenty of will-power to make up for my lack of talent. Above all, I have an enormous love of the mountains. Don't be put off either by people telling you you are too old. I get this all the time. "Oh! You're too old and should think about retiring." To hell with that! "It's not how old you are but how you are old." Nothing's impossible! Or as Mallory said: "To know there's no

dream that mustn't be dared." On my last trip to Everest I was 58 years old and got to 27,800 feet (8,340 m) without oxygen. Until the day I die I will be an explorer. My advice to you is: 'Go for it and don't let the doubters get you down."

Physical Conditioning

You certainly have to be very, very, very fit before you attempt to climb a Himalayan giant. Running is absolutely essential. You have to run and run like the Red Dogs in Kipling's novel *The Jungle Book*. Cycling and swimming too are ideal activities for getting into condition. The main emphasis must be on cardiovascular improvement. If you remember, Tenzing Norgay got fit by filling his rucksack with small rocks and climbing up steep hills around his home. Long-distance walks with a rucksack of 44 lbs (20 kg) or more will be enormously beneficial. The idea that you can get fit on the approach march to the mountain is sheer nonsense. A good level of fitness before the expedition will certainly give you the best chance of achieving the summit. It is vital that you do not 'peak-out' in fitness before the expedition but slowly increase your overall state of fitness right up to departure. Above all, you must have confidence in your physical condition. We all go through bad days during acclimatisation and it helps your

Above: *Physical conditioning prior to the climb is of vital importance to success – and survival. Brian Blessed and* Daily Mail *reporter Julian Champkin – following the hardiest traditions of journalists on Everest – make an acclimatisation trek before the ascent in 1993.*

Left: *A team work up the foot of the Lhotse Face. They are crossing a bergschrund – a crevasse at the foot of a steep slope – using a ladder and ropes.*

Right: *Our expedition leader Steve Bell. Steve has 20 years mountaineering experience behind him, including winter seasons in the Alps and three previous expeditions to the Himalayas. Steve is himself an Everest summiteer, having not just climbed, but also organised and guided an expedition in 1993.*

state of mind to know you are in excellent physical condition, and that knowledge helps you cope with this difficult phase.

Of course you have been accepted on this expedition because of your previous experience. You have completed seasons in the Alps and climbed such mountains as Aconcagua in Argentina, Elbrus in the Caucuses, Kilimanjaro and Mount Kenya in Kenya and Mount McKinley in Alaska.

I must now ask you to diligently peruse the check lists below to discover just how much you need to do, acquire and arrange before we can go on the climb. Keep your nose to the grindstone and exercise supreme patience.

The Expedition Leaders

Our expedition leader is 34-year-old Steve Bell. It is said that 'a leader must be a step above the angels', and Bell shares this distinction with the likes of Bonington, Dyrenforth and Lord Hunt. He has numerous climbs to his credit, including attempts at Everest in 1988 and 1992 with the British Services' expeditions. He led the Himalayan Kingdoms' Everest Expedition in 1993, which placed 16 people on the summit on 7 and 9

October, Steve Bell being one of the summitiers.

I was fortunate enough to be on this expedition and was able to observe Steve at first hand. He was outstanding and impressed me deeply with his skill and professionalism. He was full of care for members of the team and in moments of despair, he was always on hand with a smile and an encouraging word. When ascending the mountain he was always up front, forcing the route. When descending he was generally at the back, looking after stragglers like myself and making sure we arrived safely back at Base Camp. We all felt secure under his mantle and he was a source of inspiration for us all. My fellow adventurers, we couldn't be in better hands.

Steve has decided that our expedition will go in the spring to the mountain's North Side in Tibet. We will attempt to climb the classic North Ridge Route. That is the line that Mallory and Irvine followed in 1924. It will be a Himalayan Kingdoms' expedition. As you will have gathered, as I have climbed on Everest with them before as a paying client, I have decided that we shall go with them, because I feel that they are second to none.

Here is the outline itinerary:

The expedition will last ten weeks from 24 March until 3 June.

Day 1	Fly to Kathmandu on Royal Nepal Airlines
Day 2	Arrive Kathmandu
Day 3	At leisure
Day 4	Drive to Kodari on the Tibetan border
Day 5	Enter Tibet and drive to Nylam
Day 6-9	Acclimatisation
Day 10	Drive to Xegar
Day 11	At leisure
Day 12	Drive to Base Camp
Day 13-15	Acclimatising at Base Camp. Yaks carry equipment to Advance Base Camp
Day 19-63	Ascent of Lhakpa-Re (23,150 feet–6,945 m) and ascent of Everest
Day 64-67	Withdraw to Base Camp
Day 68-69	Drive to Kathmandu
Day 70	At leisure
Day 71	Fly from Kathmandu to London

You may be puzzled by the inclusion of Lhakpa-Re Peak (23,150 feet—6,945 m). This peak is accessible from Base Camp at 21,300 feet (6,390 m) and it is Steve's idea to use the ascent of the peak to assist acclimatisation. It will be a very serious climb in its own right, for it is higher than Aconcagua (in Argentina), the highest mountain in the Southern Hemisphere. Given reasonable weather, this plan should succeed.

Besides Steve Bell, there will be two other guides. The redoubtable Martin Barnicott, 'Barny' as he is affectionately called, is one of Britain's most respected mountain guides, and summited Everest in 1993. To complete the threesome we have the services of the outstanding Argentinian mountain guide, Daniel Alessio. Daniel has successfully climbed Cho-Oyu and Shishapangma. Ten Nepalese Sherpas will also be specially selected for their proven high altitude ability and there will also be three cooks ready to feed us at Base Camp and Advanced Base Camp.

Even with this level of support, it is a huge undertaking, requiring considerable mountaineering experience, stamina and determination. Many people have climbed Everest from the South, but only a few from the Tibetan side, i.e. the Northern Side.

The expedition will provide between 50 and 60 cylinders of oxygen. These are alloy carbon fibre wrapped cylinders that have been well tested on two earlier British Everest expeditions. The breathing apparatus is state of the art equipment, with different face masks for climbing and sleeping. Oxygen will be used from about 25,000 feet (7,500 m). Complete instructions on its use and all the relevant safety procedures will be given to us while acclimatising at Base Camp.

Well, that is a tremendous amount of information to take in. But that is the colossal amount of organisation and preparation that is required to climb Mount Everest. For a complete list of all the equipment and requirements needed for our expedition, please see the special 'Gearing up for Everest' section which begins on page 158.

MONSOON

When you climb Mount Everest you have to take into account the monsoon – a wind that carries rain originating over the Indian Ocean. Around July it blows water-laden from the south west in a north easterly direction across India, rising up the slopes and expanding and cooling as it ascends. Eventually

Below: *The monsoon snows create dangerous avalanche conditions. This is the approach to the South Face: tons of ice and snow crash off the Nuptse Ridge into the Western Cwm.*

the water vapour condenses and rain pours in torrents mainly on the southern and mid-slopes of the mountains. The great elevation of the high Himalaya provide a perpetual repository for these monsoon rains in the form of snow and glaciers, which slowly melts to feed the rivers throughout the dry season.

The monsoon dictates two periods or 'windows' as climbers call them, during which Everest can be attempted – the 'pre-monsoon' period between mid-May and mid-June and the 'post-monsoon' season between mid-September and early October. The former has become the classic time for climbing the mountain. At that time conditions are at their best with snow cover at its firmest and days which get progressively warmer.

Having said this, these conditions are never guaranteed and the weather can be atrocious. Everest is an unpredictable mountain! Once the monsoon arrives with its heavy snowfall, which can be at any time in June and sometimes even earlier, conditions on the mountain deteriorate rapidly. Though it becomes warmer the snow is deep and the risk of avalanches increases considerably. Prolonged spells of fine weather are greater in September and October, when the monsoon starts to withdraw, though it is generally colder than in the spring. In the second half of October the wind changes direction and blows from the north east, heralding winter.

Second Step

First Step

Final Pyramid and
Summit 8,863m

The Pinnacles

Camp VI
8,190m

Camp V 7,680m

North East Ridge

North Ridge

Great Couloir

Hornbein Couloir

North Col

Changtse

Camp IV
6,945m

Camp III 6,390m

East Rongbuk Glacier

Beiteng Glacier

Camp II
5,940m

North West Ridge

West Shoulder

Central Rongbuk Glacier

West Rongbuk Glacier

Base Camp I
5,100m

OUR ROUTE UP THE NORTH FACE

This is our planned route to the summit of Everest. We will be climbing the great North Face by the North Col and the North Ridge. At Camp V, we will leave the North Ridge and traverse the Face to reach the North East Ridge about 800 feet (240 m) below the First Step. If all goes well we then follow the ridge over the First and Second Steps to the final summit pyramid.

Our expedition has 54 days from our arrival at Base Camp on the Rongbuk Glacier to accomplish the climb and make a safe and successful descent. Included in our time are vitally important weeks spent acclimatising and undertaking a practice climb of the smaller peak, Lhakpe-Re. This mountain is 'only' 23,200 feet (6,960 m) high, and will be an achievement in itself. It will also help us to reach a high degree of fitness and acclimatisation for our main task.

Our expedition organisers, Himalayan Kingdoms will be in charge of setting up and supplying the six intermediate camps which will house and feed us on our ascent from the East Rongbuk Glacier to the final camp – Camp VI – which will be perched on the North Face itself. For a day-by-day breakdown of our complete ten week itinerary, please see page 84.

The North Face

Up until the 1950s, the North Face was the only part of Everest accessible to Western – or to be more precise British – mountaineers, because they had gained access to Tibet through India. Nepal on the mountain's southern side had sealed itself off from outsiders. After World War II the situation was reversed. China invaded Tibet and sealed off access to the north, while Nepal, nervous at this dangerous development sought friends beyond its borders, and in a token opened up the southern route to Everest.

It was a Chinese expedition in May 1960 that finally succeeded where Mallory and Irvine had failed, and climbed to the summit via the North Ridge route – though many in the West doubted the claim at the time.

The North Face remained closed and unclimbed until it was attempted again by the Chinese in May 1975 when they put an astonishing nine people – mostly Tibetans –

on the summit in a single assault.

The North Face was finally opened to outsiders in 1979 and was climbed by a Sino-Japanese expedition in 1980. Expedition members Tsuneo Shigehiro and Takashi Ozaki reaching the summit via the Hornbein Couloir and the West Ridge on 10 May.

The first ascent of the North Face by a mountaineer from the West took place that October and was the remarkable solo effort without oxygen by Reinhold Messner (see our final chapter 'Everest Without Oxygen' which begins on page 148).

In the last few years, the North Face route by the North Ridge has gained popularity and is being attempted by more and more expeditions. In the spring of 1995, 100 people were tackling Everest over its North Face.

While preparing for our climb and in taking stock of the many dangers we will have to overcome, it might be worthwhile to remember some of the words of George Leigh Mallory:

In all it may be said that one factor beyond all others is required for success. Too many chances are against the climbers; too many contingencies may turn against them. Anything like a breakdown of the transport will be fatal; soft snow on the mountain will be an impregnable defence; a big wind will send back the strongest; even so small a matter as a boot fitting a shade too tight may endanger one man's foot and involve the whole party in retreat. The climber must have above all things, if they are to win through, good fortune, and the greatest good fortune of all for mountaineers, some constant spirit of kindness in Mount Everest itself, the forgetfulness for long enough of its more cruel moods; for we must remember that the highest of mountains is capable of severity, a severity so awful and so fatal that the wiser sort of men do well to think and tremble even on the threshold of their high endeavour.

Now we know what awaits us, shall we make a start?

'And there are many other opportunities for adventure, whether they be sought . . . in the air, upon the sea, in the bowels of the earth, or on the ocean bed . . . There is no height, no depth, that the spirit of man, guided by a higher Spirit, cannot attain'.
JOHN HUNT, 1953[5]

THE CLIMB

I ENTREAT YOU NOW to suspend disbelief and allow your imagination to soar and join mine on this great quest to Everest. Allow me the dramatic licence to speed you along past the tedious formalities of Heathrow Airport, to the end of your 10-hour flight and arrival at Kathmandu, the magical capital of Nepal. Here you are met by your Himalayan Kingdoms' representative, who introduces you to some of the Sherpas who will be on your expedition. They greet you with garlands of white rhododendrons.

Happiness and the spirit of spring abounds. Though it is March and you are at an altitude of 4,500 feet (1,350 m), the afternoon sun is very strong and the temperature is over 70°F. The road outside the small airport is crammed with hooting taxis and the enthusiastic cyclists, who constantly ring their bells and fill the air with excited shouts. The giggling Sherpas quickly grab your rucksacks and bags and stack them on the roof of a blue bus nearby. All present and correct? Good! Then off we go, destination – the Summit Hotel.

It is amusing to observe a cow, passively chewing the cud in the middle of the roadway on the way from the airport to the city centre. The bus driver throws himself into the frantic competition that characterises Kathmandu. Don't hold your breath, breathe easy and relax. I promise there is no danger of him hitting any of the sleepy Nepalese, though I must confess I can never understand how the few traffic lights work. They all seem to go red at the same time, allowing dogs, cattle and pedestrians to cross the road in relative safety and then all

Above: *Binoculars used during the British expedition of 1936.*

Left: *On the way to the mountain. A suspension bridge across the Dudh Kosi river in the Nepalese foothills.*

Right: *An inspired leader and a constant source of guidance and advice to our expedition: our leader Steve Bell.*

change back to green in unison. Rickshaws, bicycles, trolley-buses, built in China, and battered taxis, ancient and modern grind to a noisy halt in the middle of the intersection. Then, employing great skill, they miracu- lously untangle themselves and speed off on their merry way. On all my visits to Kathmandu, I have never seen an accident. Have you ever seen so many people?

Kathmandu

Kathmandu is situated in a broad central valley and has a population of 500,000. The official language, Nepali, is derived from Sanskrit and is similar to Hindi. An early visitor once said of the capital: "Every other building is a temple, every other day is a festival."

Above: *The Summit Hotel in Kathmandu where we will spend our first days. Enjoy the luxury while you can – it won't last long.*

Right: *Colourful prayer flags festoon one of the many temples of Kathmandu. This is the main stupa at the Monkey Temple. The eyes are those of the all-seeing Buddha.*

With over 2,500 religious monuments scattered throughout the Kathmandu valley, this claim is not far off the mark; as for festivals 'every other day' is only a mild exaggeration. There are more than 50 festivals on the Nepalese calendar, totalling 120 days of celebration per year. The festivals of Nepal are authentic and are the genuine expression of the culture and religion; they are not put on solely for the tourists.

In the past, Nepal was a hidden land, now it is open to the world. In 1992 alone, it received over 334,000 tourists. Now it breathes the free atmosphere of newly nurtured democracy.

Here at last, as we ascend Kupondel heights is the Summit Hotel where we are staying, with its panoramic views of Kathmandu. It is a delightful hotel, built in the style of the Old Raj, with a terraced garden that shades you from the hot sun and catches the gentle cooling breeze from across the valley.

I know what you are thinking! We have come here to climb a mountain. All I can say is – enjoy it while you can. Things will soon get tough enough! Oh! Before you start relaxing, the hotel and Himalayan Kingdoms have laid on a special Nepali welcome. It is a sacred ceremony and is part and parcel of wishing you safety and success on the mountain. We each receive a garland of red and gold flowers and our faces are anointed with red 'tika' powder. After this we eat a specially prepared hard-boiled egg and drink distilled rice fire water. I find this simple ceremony very moving and I will allow anyone, anywhere to bless me, if it will help me to survive the savage ordeal of ascending the North Ridge of Everest.

Steve Bell has recommended that we have a meal in the famous Thamel District, which is the social centre of Kathmandu. Eating out is never a problem. There we meet the rest of the Sherpas on the expedition, including our Sirdar (foreman) the powerful Nga Temba, who has summited Everest twice. After a great evening we return to the Summit Hotel, happy and suitably weary and sleep like babies.

Our First Full Day

Good Morning! Today is a rest day. Time to check your gear and see if you need to purchase any vital item you may have forgotten from the scores of climbing equipment shops in Kathmandu. There is also time for sightseeing. Great temples are situated throughout the valley of Kathmandu and it is quite impossible to visit them all in a day. So may I recommend the Pashupatinath Temple. It is one of the most important Hindu Temples, dedicated to Lord Shiva. Statues and little shrines, some a thousand years old, are scattered along the Bagmati

River and up into the surrounding forest – a quiet, powerful place that will give you an insight into one of the world's great religions. Situated only two miles east of the centre of Kathmandu, it is a 15-minute drive by car, taxi, or you could go in a rickshaw. You have to be respectful about photographing private scenes, such as cremations or people bathing in the river. You would not wish to offend.

There is so much to see! For travellers with a thirst for adventure, Kathmandu is a starting point for wonderful trips into wildlife conservation centres, like the Royal Chitwan National Park and Parsa Wildlife Reserve or to Lumbini, the birthplace of Lord Buddha.

Journey to Tibet

After our day of relaxation, Day 3 sees us setting off for

Below: *Pagoda roofs in Kathmandu.*

Bottom: *Market day in bustling Namche Bazaar, the capital of the Solo Khumbu.*

Tibet. Our two large trucks are packed with 4½ tons of equipment, and after an hour or so, off we go, heading for Friendship Bridge, which spans the border between Nepal and Tibet. Honking and hooting, we make our way through the Nepalese countryside. We pass the mysterious splendours of ancient Bhaktapur and drive along glorious tree-lined roads that lead the way to the great mountains.

The soil of the Kathmandu Valley is deep red in colour, which accounts for the pretty red brick buildings that dot the hillside. The whole country seems alive with villagers waving and cheering us along.

The haze of early morning has started to clear, revealing the intricate patterns of the many rice-fields, where beautiful black-eyed women in vibrant dresses of green, yellow, blue and red, toil away rhythmically.

Having ascended gradually, we stop for breakfast at a charming wooden hillside restaurant. We marvel at an astonishing 200° panorama of Himalayan peaks. In hushed tones, our leader points out some of the mountains: Ganesh, Himal Chuli, Shishapangma, Gaurishankar and Menlungtse. "Where is Everest?" We all whisper impatiently. "You can't see it from here," replies one of the Sherpas. "It's way, way over there, deep in the interior. You'll see it in a few days."

After breakfast we are back on the road. Down, down, down we now go into the patchwork patterns of the walled fields. The valley is steeper and the electric green of the newly sprouted rice fields gives way to spectacular rough crags carved by the devastating power of the water from the mountains, which ultimately will form the Indus and the Ganges rivers.

Below: *A Sherpa girl sits in front of the oven in a tea house in Pangboche.*

Above: *The Himalayas are home to some spectacular birds, including the enormous Himalayan Griffon, seen here perched in front of Everest herself. The Griffon can have a wingspan of 8 feet (2.5 m), and can soar upwards to altitudes of 19,000 feet (5,700 m).*

charging you large amounts in sterling or US dollars for doing so. Be that as it may, let's just grin and bear it and unpack our bags for inspection yet again.

With a sigh of relieve, we are given the 'official nod' and allowed to cross the bridge. Our two trucks now turn around and go back to Nepal; our vehicles henceforth will be rented from the Chinese authorities.

After a couple of hours' waiting with our equipment, we give a mighty cheer as Steve Bell arrives with a huge lorry and a Tibetan driver. Now we load up and trundle up the hill to have our credentials checked. This boring rigmarole of customs, passports and visas takes about three hours. We are finally allowed to pass on to the huge and depressing Xangu Hotel. This is supposed to be a first class hotel but is actually a frightful place. Our rooms are damp and cold and the pathetic electrical fittings hang loosely from the walls. The evening meal, in a large hall, is frugal and plain, yet reasonably nourishing. Anyway, who gives a damn! Tomorrow we will be moving deep into Tibet, the fabled Land of Bo.

Into Tibet

We wake up excited and raring to go. The plan is simple. Daniel Alessio and several Sherpas will press ahead with the lorry and set up Base Camp, whilst we arrive later in two Toyota Land Cruisers. It is staggering to think that when Mallory and his companions approached Everest in 1921, it took them three months from Darjeeling to get to Base Camp, a distance of 300 miles (480 km). We, on the other hand, will arrive in a matter of days. Our Land Cruisers are very comfortable and we make rapid progress. But we must be very careful to acclimatise, for we have come from 4,500 feet to 8,000 feet (1,350–2,400 m) very quickly. We stop frequently, get out and walk around for a while, and then resume our journey.

The towering cliffs overlooking the rough road along which we are motoring are stunning and intimidating. We find ourselves travelling under a gigantic rocky overhang with thousands of tons of water thundering over it into the great gorge below. As much as one resents a road in such a wild place, one has to admit that the Chinese and Tibetans have done an amazing job constructing it.

Now as we leave the awesome splendour of the rocky cliffs and ravines below, we find ourselves on the Tibetan Plateau at 10,000 feet (3,000 m). After being hemmed in by the previous massive structures, it is a complete surprise to find ourselves gazing for hundreds of miles over a multi-coloured desert. There is a great variety of colour in the sand and the rock and we stand together in a vast, sandy plain with gentle distant mountains all around us, that for all the world look 'Martian' in character.

Friendship Bridge

On reaching Friendship Bridge, we are eager to get across and into Tibet, but there is also sadness at having to leave Nepal. The Chinese border guards on the bridge look none too friendly and Steve Bell instructs us to do exactly as they tell us. We must nod, smile, bow and scrape and raise not a finger in contention. They can keep us here on the bridge for days or weeks if they wish. It is not easy, for the Chinese can be deliberately obstructive but, if we lose our tempers, we could place the whole expedition in jeopardy.

Two of the Chinese officers on the bridge are representatives of the Chinese Mountaineer Association – the CMA. The CMA governs every attempt on Everest in Tibet, solving problems of their own making and

Right: *Our crossing place into Tibet – the Friendship Bridge. The view is from the Tibetan side looking back into Nepal. The line in the middle of the bridge is the official border.*

Below: *A sight that is now very rare in the Himalayas. The beautiful Snow Leopard has almost been hunted to extinction for its coat.*

Left: *As we move deeper into Tibet we can look back towards the Himilaya, having just driven through them from Nepal. We are lucky, we have motors, the first British expeditions had to walk — and there were no roads.*

The dust-infested westerly wind of Tibet, often described as 'the old wind with the old anger' is thankfully not blowing and all is stillness and harmony. The thin air allows our eyes to see the full depth of the rich cobalt blue of the sky. The striking colour highlights the soft pinks and beiges of the smooth hills, as they roll on and on to the distant azure and deep purple of the floating heights of the Himalayas. Taking in the kisses of the laughing Sun is the mighty presence of the great mountain, Shishapangma. In the far distance a herd of yaks are being urged on by a woolly-hatted herdsman.

Captain Noel who first entered Tibet in 1913, felt that, despite its charm, Tibet is unquestionably the most desolate country in the world. He explained to me once that: "No other land can be so harsh and forbidding as that roof of the world, raised 15,000 feet (4,500 m), where stone and ice and mountain seem to conspire against life. The people live in the most extreme poverty and discomfort, yet, they are contented and happy."

Well, the powerful sun is losing its strength and it is time to climb back into the Cruiser and head for the small town of Nylam, at about 12,500 feet (3,750 m), where we will stay the night. On arrival we are informed by the CMA that they have booked us into a hotel where the charge will be $85 per person for bed, breakfast and evening meal. It is an appalling place, isn't it? You can hardly call it a hotel. With no heating in sub-zero temperatures, it looks more like a concrete barracks. Oh! If only we were back at the Summit Hotel in Kathmandu!

The evening meal is guaranteed to be dreadful, so Steve Bell will pass you a supply of goodies from our food stocks to cheer you up. The main thing now is to take it easy, because for the first time we are above 12,000 feet (3,600 m). Your blood is beginning to thicken, as the red blood cells increase. Remember to drink as much liquid as you can. Steve and the expedition doctor recommend that you take an aspirin before you go to sleep in your sleeping bag.

Below: *At the snow line at 15,000 feet (4,500 m) we stop and look across the barren plateau towards the great peak Shishapangma.*

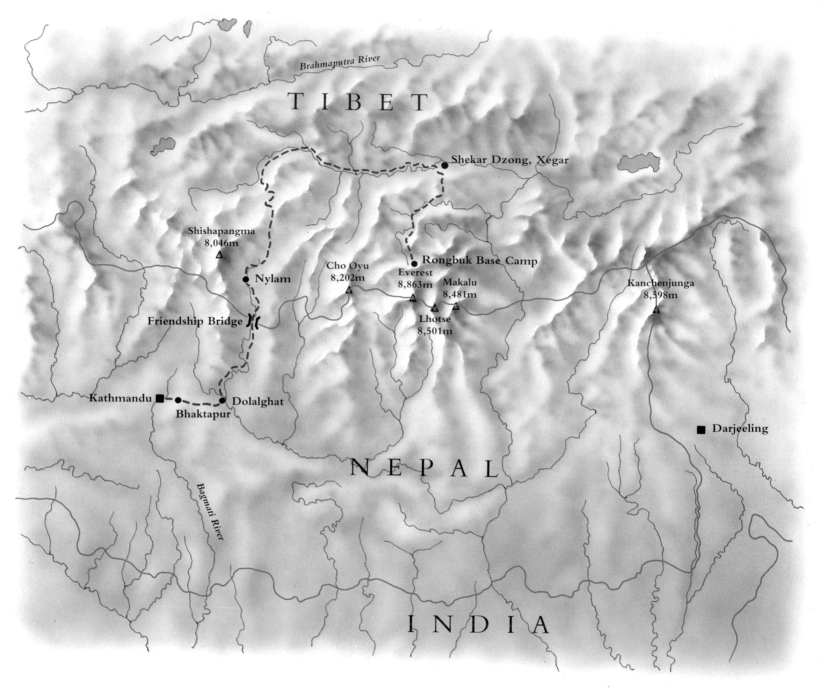

On the map:

Brahmaputra River

T I B E T

Shekar Dzong, Xegar

Shishapangma
8,046m

Cho Oyu
8,202m

Rongbuk Base Camp

Nylam

Everest
8,863m

Makalu
8,481m

Kanchenjunga
8,598m

Lhotse
8,501m

Friendship Bridge

Kathmandu

Dolalghat

Bhaktapur

Darjeeling

N E P A L

Bagmati River

I N D I A

Above: *Our route from Kathmandu to Everest Base Camp. Travelling mostly along river valleys, we move north across the Friendship Bridge, up through the Himalaya. We only turn back towards the south near Xegar, to approach the Everest Massif from the north.*

The Tibetan Interior

The following morning, after a leisurely breakfast, we climb once more into our Land Cruisers and set off for our next port of call, Xegar. We welcome the warmth of the vehicle, for there is a cold breeze and the temperature is well below zero. Despite the cold, great lammergeiers are already circling overhead and choughs and ravens squawk excitedly, as they devour the tit-bits that we have left for them. It is said that the air in Tibet is so dry that meat will keep for years without going rotten. It is so cold and the land so poor, that the only crop that can grow successfully is barley.

Over there you can see a party of women digging. The digging is always done by two people with one wooden spade. One pushes the spade slowly by the handle and the other pulls it with a rope. At 15,000 feet (4,500 m) above sea level, manual labour is a strain on the heart even for Tibetans.

On and on we drive across the rugged contours of the wind-ravaged steppes of the Ancient Land of Bo. This lofty, mystical kingdom has tantalised explorers and travellers for thousands of years. We leave the Cruiser to walk for a while once more. Do you not think that this is the solitude you yearned for as a child? Bite back at the fierce wind and wipe your tear-filled eyes and look on the distant peaks bathed in the early morning sun. Is this indeed the first day of the rest of your life? Yes, you are hooked, drugged, blissed out by the humming song of the Himalayas. And higher, stronger, louder than this song is the siren call of 'The Goddess Mother Of The Earth', Mount Everest – less than 100 miles (160 km) from where you are standing. Closer, closer. Oh, we are getting ever so close. Let us retire back into the security of our Cruisers and motor on towards our hearts desire.

Hours later, as darkness enfolds us, we approach historic Xegar. Before the Chinese invasion of Tibet in 1950, Xegar was known as Shekar Dzong. Now, as we arrive, it is completely dark and torches are in use everywhere. Stern-faced Tibetan matrons who seem put out that we have arrived so late show us to our rooms. We are now at 14,000 feet (4,200 m) and are interested only in getting our heads down and trying to sleep. Because of the intense cold we put on our fleece-lined duvets, make ourselves comfortable and, after eating a couple of hard-boiled eggs and a bar of chocolate, settle into our sleeping bags and pray for sleep.

The following morning is cold and bright and I leave my cell-like room and cross the passage to join you peering out of one of the many windows. There, catching the first rays of the sun, are the majestic ruins of Shekar Dzong, rising to a height of over 15,000 feet (4,500 m).

The Dzong Pens, or Lords of Tibet, in the early days of the century, described it as the 'Shining White Glass Fort', because of its complex of gleaming white monastery buildings and hermit cells that cling like honeycombs to the side of the hill and dominate the village. Four hundred monks lived here in those days. On the hilltop was a medieval fortress. What a desecration of a harmonious and sacred way of life! How could anyone reduce to ruins the once proud fort, with its luminously

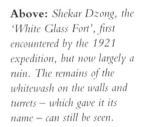

Above: *Shekar Dzong, the 'White Glass Fort', first encountered by the 1921 expedition, but now largely a ruin. The remains of the whitewash on the walls and turrets – which gave it its name – can still be seen.*

Left: *The view from the fort at about 15,200 feet (4,560 m), looking down on to the town of Shekar. Some of the fort's ruined towers can be seen on the left.*

beautiful white terraced buildings. Because of the fort's altitude, the Chinese used tanks, mortar bombs and Mig fighter planes, which pounded at its fortifications for days on end. Four hundred monks prayed and meditated in a special room on the summit, as the enemy snarled and tore away the very fabric of their way of life. All is rubble now. Yet no desecration can rob it of its natural majesty, for the skeletal remains possess a dignity that survives all. The monks and nuns have returned, albeit but a few, and the slow process of renovation has begun.

Anyway, once more to our own activities, for breakfast beckons. The Ding Ri County Hotel, proudly proclaims that its standards are equal to those of a four star hotel. Steve Bell adds ruefully that at $150 a night, only its prices are! On the wall is a certificate awarding the hotel a Chinese Michelin star. I believe that two of our lady climbers have already paid the price for having early breakfast and have spent the morning retching in the

latrines. I think it is advisable to wait for some of our own cooking. Steve has asked with maximum courtesy if they would mind our cook, Krisna, preparing food from our own supplies, to which the Chinese chef has reluctantly agreed. Twenty minutes later we are tucking into cheese omelettes and chunks of fresh bread.

Acclimatisation

For the next two days we must employ great patience and sit about and take it easy. We have arrived at 14,000 feet (4,200 m) in a very short space of time and we have to allow our bodies to adjust to the altitude. I have always felt that this height is very important. It is the half-way mark in the ascent of Everest. If climbers rush impatiently past it in an endeavour to gain height rapidly, they seem to pay for it later. Higher up, they frequently become sluggish and disappointed in their performance.

Let us assume now that the two days have passed.

Below: *A Tibetan carrying a prayer wheel. Inside the wheel is a consecrated written mantra, and each turn of the wheel is meant to be the equivalent of a recitation of that mantra. Written mantras are also placed on prayer flags to be moved by the wind.*

Today, the fourth and final day we spend at Shekar Dzong, we test our lungs and climb to the top of the ruins of the fort to a height of 15,200 feet (4,560 m). The weather is fine, with only a mild breeze, and the scenery is absolutely breath-taking.

Starting from the base at 14,000 feet (4,200 m), we begin slowly to move upwards. That's the idea. Slowly, slowly. Watch Steve Bell, he doesn't take long steps but little ones, to conserve energy. Just concentrate on your breathing – in and out, nice and easy does it. Gently settle into a comfortable natural rhythm, there's no rush. We rush so much in the West, don't we? Good, you are all doing fine. It is amazing isn't it? We are not going fast and yet it is remarkable how much height we have gained, probably about 500 feet. Take care here, the fragile rocks on the steep sections require delicate handling.

It becomes quite tricky now, as we climb the almost vertical hillside and pull ourselves through a broken wall and into a roofless meditation room. We are all totally stunned and speechless. We have arrived at 15,200 feet (4,560 m). The craggy walls bear witness to the shells that have hit them and the gaping holes reveal the town and patterned emerald barley fields far, far below. The scarcity of air is more noticeable now because the incessant icy wind takes our breath away. The ruined room bewitches our senses with its holy offerings. Zip, zip, zip, – the wind peppers the hundreds of coloured prayer flags. Its wild energy kisses every vestige of these fluttering butterflies and carries their message of love from that roofless room on the roof of the world to mankind and the heavens beyond. It is wonderful to be here with you all, sharing the experience. Aren't we lucky? Just think, this is where General Bruce, Mallory and Captain Noel came. They were greeted by the Dzong Pen, way down there in a little walled garden surrounded by willow trees, where

Below: *Tibetan mani stones. These are natural stones on which Sanskrit prayers have been carved. As a religious observance, mani stones and walls must always be approached from the left.*

they were given sweetmeats, flowers and gifts.

What a view we have my friends, as we stand on top of one of the more secure walls. Hundreds and hundreds of miles of undulating mountainous desert. The sinking Sun's rays plunge the whole vision into an unbelievable sea of searing scarlet, that transforms the azure sky into pink.

Our First Sight of Everest

The following afternoon, after a short journey in the Cruiser, we disembark to experience once again a sunset of miraculous intensity. The stillness and silence is almost unnerving. Everest is so close now, so tantalizingly close. We all sense it but so far, amazingly, we have seen nothing of it. In this almost surrealistic golden afternoon light, we feel that we are in a dream landscape. The setting sun paints the hills with subtle pastel shades of red and pink that deepen and herald the appearance of the 'Goddess Mother of the Earth'.

With Steve leading the way, we slither and crawl up to the 16,800 foot (5,040 m) 'Pang La' (The Grassy Col) and witness a vision that for starkness, grandeur and majesty, dwarfs all our imagining. "Everest! Everest!" we whisper in scarcely suppressed excitement. Then our emotions explode and we dance and leap about in an incoherent celebration of life, life that emanates from that colossal, beatific symbol of all that is inspirational in nature. "It's Everest. Look at the size of it! It's so steep! It's so massive. It looks like the end of the world. As if there is nothing beyond it!"

You're right my friends, it looks so massive, like a gigantic cathedral built by the gods! In our ravings we

Facing page: *Whilst driving across the Tibetan plateau, we get our first view of Everest. Now we start to realise its immense scale, and the enormous challenge we have set ourselves. We are still 70 miles (112 km) away and yet the mountain rises up, dominant and implacable.*

Above: *If Everest wasn't intimidating enough, there are many other peaks that vie for our attention. This is the gigantic bulk of Cho-Oyu. Its characteristic shape can also be seen on the extreme right of the main photograph.*

sound like people who have taken leave of their senses, which is perfectly understandable. Quite apart from Everest, our blitzed minds are attempting to take in the 100-mile-wide panorama of the Himalayas. There alongside the great mountain is Changse, The North Peak, mighty Makalu and glittering white Cho-Oyu. Giants and more giants stretching out endlessly. Steve says: "The whole mountain is glowing. It feels like a friend. I can't wait to get up there – just to look at those colours. Looks steep though. This is it, ladies and gentlemen, this is 'the big one'!"

An hour later we all sit close together, utterly blissed out. The wonders of the day are not over, for, as the sun is on the point of disappearing, Everest and the surrounding mountains turn a deep burgundy red.

As darkness enfolds us we approach the tiny village of Tingri and spend the night there.

The Turquoise Mountain

The next morning we head for Base Camp. We are now only 30 miles (48 km) from the mountain. For the first time I can understand why Everest has been named by the ancients 'The Turquoise Mountain'. In the early morning sunlight there is no division between the mountain and sky. Everest appears to be floating in the heavens, its rocks are dark turquoise and its snow fields are just a shade lighter. Clouds from below occasionally obscure the view and for the first time, we cast eyes on Everest's famous 'streamer'. The powerful west wind tears at its summit, carrying tiny ice crystals in a stream stretching for miles. Climbers dread this, as it signifies that conditions are severe for summit attempts. We are drawn to the mountain like a magnet, as we move slowly onward.

The Land Cruisers now prove their worth, as they bounce and bump their way across rocky terrain. We now find ourselves deep in the Rongbuk Valley; with soaring peaks all around us we are quite unable to see Everest. The road is strewn with boulders and the Cruisers have difficulty in coping. We all feel a bit battered and disembark and decide to walk for a while. We round a corner and find ourselves looking at a few low-lying white and red buildings with green roofs. We blink and stare at it all. Our brains are working slowly, as if in a slow-motion dream, for we are looking at possibly the most breathtaking sight on Earth. We are standing at 16,400 feet (4,920 m) above sea level and in front of us is the highest monastery in the world: the legendary Rongbuk Monastery.

Look! The valley, more than a mile wide, runs directly ahead for nearly 20 miles (32 km). At its far end, filling the valley with its gargantuan North Face of granite and

Previous pages: *We are now at 16,400 feet (4,920 m) and experiencing perhaps the finest view on this Earth. Chomolungma – the Goddess Mother – rises up like some vast natural cathedral in front of the world's highest monastery, the Rongbuk.*

These pages: *Here is our goal at last. Dominating the broad sweep of the desolate Rongbuk Valley stands the enormity of Everest's great North Face, with the East Rongbuk Glacier running off to our left. This is the end of our journey, but just the beginning of the greater adventure. In a few short hours we will be at the very foot of the mountain at Everest Base Camp.*

snow, is Everest. Behind the modest structure of the monastery, nature's genius has completed the picture with a hall of grandeur that leads to the mountain. We all sink to our knees and remain motionless. To think that Captain Noel, in 1913, after three previous attempts, got to within 40 miles of Everest. It had been rumoured for years that the monastery existed. Captain Noel finally found it in 1922. Well, we are having the privilege of seeing it now. Everest, viewed from here, does look very intimidating and I can see that the sight of it overwhelms you.

"It looks terrifying!"

"We are suffering from headaches at just 16,000 feet [4,800m]. What will it be like when we get higher? What if we fail to get up the East Rongbuk Glacier and stop at 20,000 feet [6,000 m]?"

"What do you think, Steve?" I ask.

"I think we should all relax and play it cool and take it one step at a time," replies our unperturbed leader.

I am afraid that the Rongbuk Monastery has suffered the same fate as Shekar Dzong. In 1922 there were hundreds of monks and nuns at Rongbuk, resplendent in ceremonial robes and fantastic masks, as they danced for hours in honour of Mallory and his companions. Thank goodness that Captain Noel has put it all on film for future generations to see. Yet hope springs eternal. A Lama and a small contingent of monks and nuns are still in residence here and are beginning renovation work, which bodes well for the future.

According to Tibetan history, the great Indian saint, Padmasambhava, after travelling the Himalayas, rested a while at the monastery, on his mission to bring Buddhism to Tibet. It is said that he ascended Everest, sitting in his chair and transported by a sun-beam. It would seem that Hillary and Tenzing were not the first to ascend Everest.

We meet the Lama, and present him with a splendid 'Thangka' from His Holiness The Dalai Lama in Dharamsala. The Lama is overcome and bestows white scarves of blessing around our shoulders. His face is dark, almost purple and strong and criss-crossed with deep lines, while his eyes are full of kindness and merriment. His face lights up even further with happiness, when Steve Bell informs him, through a translator, that he will give him our surplus food once the expedition is over. Then the dreaded Tibetan tea is served. The appaling brew is terribly sweet and topped with rancid butter. To refuse a cup will be, at the very least, impolite. Whatever you do, don't gulp it down too quickly or your cup will be refilled immediately. If you really can't face drinking it, perhaps you would like to try the excuse that General

Bruce used in 1922, when he said: "Tibetan buttered tea is the most delicious tea in the world but I have taken a vow not to drink it until I have climbed Mount Everest."

Above: *The people who live in the shadow of the mountain – two yak herders in traditional dress.*

To Base Camp

It is time for us to wend our way back to our Cruiser and complete the last leg of our journey to Base Camp. Fifteen minutes later, after the bumpiest ride ever, we arrive at Base Camp at 17,000 feet (5,100 m), our highest point to date.

Daniel Alessio, Martin Barnicott, Nga Temba and the other Sherpas have done an excellent job in setting up

be done. Of course it means that we will be 'peeing' for much of the time but that's the price you have to pay. If you are not peeing regularly then it means that you are not drinking enough and that is serious. Dehydration is a very serious matter at these heights and you simply cannot drink too much. Though you do not appear to be sweating, you are, because the dry atmosphere of the high altitude draws liquid out of your body. So drink, even when you are not thirsty or you will reduce your chances of going high. It is very important now to take it easy. You should at all times listen carefully to the advice of the leader and his guides.

I am delighted to see that a toilet has been made! It fills me with relief for, in the past, it is a job that has frequently been delegated to me. Barny informs us that it is the best 'toilet' ever constructed on Everest and I must say I heartily congratulate him. It is not easy to dig a pit through shale and frozen rock, but after several hours work, the Sherpas have managed to create a decent-sized hole about four feet deep. The positioning is quite glorious. As you squat over the hole, nimbly balancing on overhanging rocks, you get the most spectacular view of Everest! Not quite the Summit Hotel but the erection of a system of flags to warn others that the toilet is occupied is the final touch of luxury that marks our expedition as being first class! By the way, ignore any giggling yak herders, who may be 'clocking' you and be careful not to fall in.

Base Camp has seen a lot of expeditions over the past ten years and they have all left their mark. It is not a pretty sight. Broken bottles and tin cans litter the moraine above our tents, and one of our expedition's

Above: *Packing up food for Base Camp. Our expedition will be taking over 1,240 lbs (565 kg) of food, not including special dehydrated, high-altitude, meals and any local produce. Our provisions will include 352 lbs (160 kg) of tinned foods. So important is fluid intake at high altitude that our provisions will also include 66 lbs (30 kg) of assorted tea, coffee and malted milk and chocolate drinks.*

Base Camp and cheerfully greet and escort us to the large yellow Litchfield mess tent, which will be the centre of our lives for the next nine weeks. Whilst the Base Camp cook, Krisna, plies us with mugs of hot coffee laced with condensed milk, Martin Barnicott explains the layout of the camp. We each have the luxury of our own Wild Country Hyperspace tents, which are red in colour and cheer the flat landscape around the mess tent.

After a couple of hours unpacking our gear and settling into our individual homes, we emerge for more mugs of coffee. We are urged to drink up to six litres of liquid a day, which is quite an undertaking, but it must

objectives will be to clear up as much rubbish as we can and take it back to Nepal, where it can be destroyed or re-cycled.

The plan now is to rest and acclimatise here for five days. During this time we will receive instruction in the use of the oxygen apparatus and the radios. There will also be an opportunity to walk alongside the terminal moraine of the Central Rongbuk Glacier up to a height of about 18,000 feet (5,400 m). Though we are not high on the mountain, this is a crucial phase in the expedition and Steve and Barny repeatedly emphasise the importance of not over-doing it. Rest and patience are now required.

I can see that this is good news, for quite a few of you have already developed chesty coughs and are experiencing a certain amount of lethargy. The smallest movement leaves you panting and gasping for breath and headaches are commonplace. The best remedy is to

Far left, top: *The yak is an ox that has adapted itself extremely successfully to high altitudes, so much so that it lives with difficulty below 10,000 feet (3,000 m). The yak can live and work at altitudes of up to 21,000 feet (6,000 m).*

Far left, bottom: *The yak of the type we will be seeing a lot of is the domestic variety, usually piebald black and white, which have been crossed with cattle. It can nevertheless carry 110 lbs (50 kg) of stores with ease.*

Right: *A Tibetan farmer spinning yak wool. The yaks are vitally important to the peoples of the Himalaya. Not only are they beasts of burden and a source of wealth, they also supply wool, meat and milk.*

Above: *At altitude it is important to rest whenever you can – taking the characteristics of the tortoise, not the hare.*

Facing page: *Rongbuk Base Camp in bad weather. Temperatures here can fall to 20 degrees below zero. Tackling the northern side of Everest, expeditions experience colder and windier conditions than those on the southern side.*

simply take an aspirin and lie still on your sleeping bag.

Most people these days have a 'Walkman' and they certainly prove their worth on expeditions like this, where there is a great deal of time to kill. We have all brought a good selection of literature and, when we finish one book, it is placed on the communal shelf in the mess tent for someone else to enjoy. It is amusing to note that on the 1922 Expedition, when Mallory and Somerville shared a tent at Camp III, they read Shakespeare to each other and played cards.

Dangers of Altitude

When I was last here, in 1990, making our film on Mallory with the BBC, we had an alarming experience with our cook. He too was called Krisna and was a sweet cheerful little fellow. On our second day at Base Camp he became ill and we had to call on the services of an American doctor called Kurt from the nearby International Peace Climb. Krisna had a fever, cramps and his heart was beating very fast. Oxygen and injections were administered but we were fearful for his life. At this altitude a simple malady can be fatal, as the bodies defences are at their weakest.

The good doctor spent the night by his side and, as dawn broke, the injections and oxygen did the trick. The little Sherpa's life was saved but it had been a near thing. One of the International climbers developed a thrombosis in his leg and a powerful woman climber on the same expedition had to be taken down to Kathmandu with clots on her lungs. To top it all, a super fit Soviet climber suffered from pulmonary oedema – all very depressing. I sound rather like the Yorkshire comedian who used to

Above: *The Lama of the Rongbuk Monastery conducting the Puja before an ascent in 1988. The Lama in 1924 was a reincarnation of the god Shongrashe. The Lama above – if he is a god – frequently suffers from toothache and loves popcorn. Given a box of asparin he'll be a friend for life.*

say: "It's being so cheerful that keeps me going."

My friends, I do not impart these stories to be sensational but to add weight to what Steve and Barny have been saying. Rest is of paramount importance if the body is to adjust successfully to the new altitude.

One or two of you are to ascend a small hill above the mess tent in the company of Steve. May I join you? Goodness, how the wind intensifies, after an ascent of only 100 feet (30 m). Here we are, hugging each other for warmth. Three quarters of Everest is in darkness, with the summit pyramid scarlet red in the evening sun. Once the sun leaves the sky, the Rongbuk Valley's temperature will plummet well below freezing, forcing us to scurry for cover and warmth. That moment is almost upon us!

"I think I will retire to bed," says Steve and descends to the mess tent, with us in hot pursuit. Oh, lovely! Isn't

it cosy in here. Take your boots off and place your feet close to the half dozen or so gas cookers. What bliss. Have you noticed that our main topic of conversation is food? We are becoming very basic and primitive!

After dinner we wish each other goodnight and set off for our tents, bracing ourselves against the freezing night air. Our eyeballs go stiff with cold and the rest of our body follows suit. With head-mounted torches flashing, we dash for cover. But I'm afraid you have to steel yourselves to have a pee before you can retire. Groans from all sides: "What are we doing in this awful place?"

The task completed you find yourself, your fingers tingling with cold, opening the reluctant zip of the inner tent. You are now a heap of shivering jelly. Having zipped up both the outer and inner flaps, you are still freezing and you talk to yourself and sing breathlessly, as you struggle to get your coat off and joyfully dive into

your huge sleeping bag. Your head-torch lights up the interior of your tent, which is covered in ice, and you listen to the strong wind that blows down the valley from the Black Goddess and shakes your tent's foundations. Sweet dreams!

The following morning, after breakfast, we move a couple of hundred yards up the valley and take in the view. The wind is really cold today and makes our eyes water. Everest towers in the sky. I have never seen it look so gigantic. What a 'hall of grandeur' leads the way to the mountain. It is a spectacle of astounding beauty and strangeness. We can't get used to its size. Everyday it surprises us. Mallory wrote in 1921: "Everest has become something more than a fantastic vision . . . the problem of its great ridges and glaciers begins to take shape mentally . . . suffice it to say that it has the most stupendous ridges and precipices that I have ever seen."

From where we are standing, we can clearly see that Everest's North Face is in the grip of a terrible hurricane-like storm, with winds from its jet stream scouring its ramparts. Steve senses our fear and tells us, "You have nothing to fear but your fear . . . you will be fine on the mountain. Don't be concerned about the bad weather. We will co-ordinate our ascents to the high camps, with decent breaks in the conditions."

With Steve's reassuring words ringing in our ears, I would like to speed our expedition along.

Imagine, my friends, that you have completed your full acclimatisation programme, which means that all the Camps are in place on Everest – the highest point being Camp Six at 27,300 feet (8,190 m) on the North Face. In the company of Steve Bell, Martin Barnicott and myself you have successfully climbed the Lhakpa-Re at 23,200 feet (6,960 m) and after this splendid achieve-

Above: Thirty yaks would normally be used in an expedition of our size, with one herder per three yaks. Even with the size of load weighing down this animal, a yak can still make a steady climb at 3 mph (4.8 km/h).

ment, we have once more retired to Base Camp for seven days to rest.

After this rest period is over, it is time for us to attempt our climb of Everest. First things first, though. The day before we go we must attend the Puja, a sacred ceremony conducted by the Lama of the Rongbuk Monastery, which invokes the blessings of certain deities. Nga Temba and all the Sherpas have done a wonderful job fixing all the pretty coloured prayer flags to string and attaching them to poles and ski sticks. It is a short, moving ceremony with the Lama and a monk taking turns to chant the prayers. At the climax of the ceremony we stand and throw rice into the air and cheer and shout. This jolly ceremony now gives us protection from misfortune and with the mountain looking radiant and red in the background, we are all deeply grateful to be able to make our peace with the Goddess, before our attempt to reach her summit.

Our Ascent Begins

At 7.00 a.m. the following day, 27 April, we all gather ready for the off. We are trying to keep calm but our eyes betray our inner excitement. Mallory once said of Everest: "Lord, when I think of it, something bubbles up inside me. The effervescence is sternly repressed, of course . . . and then a bubble outs and bursts." We have come a long way and it is a joy to arrive at this moment. Steve gives the nod and we are off.

At last we are going up the mountain to heights that we have never reached before. The Sherpas smile and laugh. It starts to snow and we put on our windproofs. We are in great spirits and move joyously across the plain, towards the terminal moraine of the Central Rongbuk Glacier. Everest, which has been hidden because of the swirling snow, suddenly reveals itself.

I am afraid that I am getting a little too excited and I feel a restraining hand from Barny on my shoulder, "Don't go so fast, Brian!" Steve nods in agreement and I exercise greater restraint but, my goodness, I am thumpingly happy! Our breathing is smoother now, even though our hearts are skipping a beat.

We are at 17,500 feet (5,250 m), a quarter of a mile up the glacier. The first rays of the morning sun begin to filter through and, miraculously, it ceases to snow and the weather becomes quite clear. We are walking up a rough, narrow path to the left of the glacier. The cliffs on that side are light brown and look like sandstone. To our right is the boulder-strewn lip of the glacier. After a few hundred yards we move on to the rim of the glacier, again following a natural path. The weather is fine and

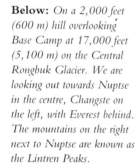

Below: *On a 2,000 feet (600 m) hill overlooking Base Camp at 17,000 feet (5,100 m) on the Central Rongbuk Glacier. We are looking out towards Nuptse in the centre, Changste on the left, with Everest behind. The mountains on the right next to Nuptse are known as the Lintren Peaks.*

Left: *Our expedition depends on the remarkable ability of the yak to work at high altitude. Loaded with our stores, these animals make their way along the terminal moraine of the East Rongbuk Glacier – known to expeditions as the 'Magik Highway' – at 20,000 feet (6,000 m) towards Advance Base Camp. Behind them are the strange 'Shark's Fins' – or penidentes – of ice, a characteristic formation of the glacier.*

still - the mountain is smiling on us and drawing us on. Another mile and we stop to have our first drink. The adjustable ski sticks that we are using are helping us to achieve a natural rhythm.

The glacier takes our breath away. It goes on and on for miles, with what look like thousands of white and green fins of ice that vary in size from 5 to 100 feet in height. They look like sharks and dolphins frozen in a white sea by the power of Everest itself. From a distance of 12 miles (19 km) we can clearly see the Hornbein Couloir, the West Ridge and the beauty of the Lingtren Peaks. It is so still; the glacier makes no sound. Only by straining our ears can we hear the distant moaning of the streamer, high on Everest. Some of you have tears in your eyes; I hear one of you whisper the words of the wise Skanda Purana: "As the dew is dried up by the morning sun, so are the sins of men dried up by the sight of the Himalaya, where Shiva lived and where the Gangu falls from the foot of Vishnu, like the slender thread of a Lotus flower."

On and on we go, deeper into the glacier, until we arrive at the historic point that is the entrance to the East Rongbuk Glacier. Here we ascend 300 feet (90 m) up a very steep cliff. The first time we attempted it was four weeks ago, before we were acclimatised and we found

the going pretty awful. Now we find it much easier, though it still makes us pant. Steve and Barny remind us constantly to conserve our energy. Now that we have turned into the East Rongbuk Glacier, our view of Everest is cut off by the high cliffs. It will be quite a while before we see it again.

We are now at 18,000 feet (5,400 m) and apart from the occasional cough, here and there, everyone is doing fine. After a slight descent into the valley of the meandering glacier, we arrive at a stream of pure uncontaminated water, drink our fill and top up our water bottles. Seduced by the scenery, we feast our eyes on the increasing size of the glacier. Even at this height the glacier reveals tiny grasses and lichen on its sides and you will see the occasional tortoiseshell butterfly.

Now we must make our way delicately across the sea of punctured ice to the other side. This is a tricky operation and Steve leads the way, with us following on behind and Barny bringing up the rear. All the while, underneath our footsteps, the icy torrent roars dangerously; it is not a place to hang about. Now that this obstacle has been overcome, we climb around many dust wells, which require great care, before we can reach the crucial hills leading to Camp II.

Though we are well acclimatised, we are still finding

this tough going. It is extraordinary how the hammering of the heart seems to carry the same rhythm as the brain, don't you think? Your entire body pounds unnervingly. We have to stop frequently to rest and for further intakes of water. Barney is right behind us, giving us encouragement. We remain cheerful and are making good progress. Everyone is free of headaches, sore throats and colds, as we approach 19,000 feet (5,700 m). We have been climbing for three hours and the sun is scorching. Thank God we have Factor 25 on our faces and lips. Once more it is time to drink some water and take off our outer wind-proof garments.

Steve and Barney give us the nod and it is time to move off again. We hoist our rucksacks on our backs and move on feeling greatly refreshed. The valley starts to widen to over a mile, with the glacier growing to embrace it, rising majestically to form the beginning of the most amazing 'Ice Kingdom' on earth. Camp II is situated on a hill overlooking a glacier stream and suitably distant from the avalanche-prone rock cliffs away to our right. We walk on a circular route below these intimidating cliffs and then down 200 yards (180 m) to finally arrive at Camp II at 19,800 feet (5,940 m).

It is mid-day and Steve decides that it is a good time to have lunch. Out come our little parcels of boiled eggs, fruit and chocolate. Our water supplies are holding out well and should last until we reach Camp III at 21,300 feet (6,390 m) – our intended destination for today. Above us is the region of ice and snow, the Kingdom of King Cold. A quick glance at the sky reassures us that the weather promises to remain good and after 15 minutes we are on our way again.

Crossing the Glacier

A steepish 200-foot (60 m) ascent over ice and scree now follows and we arrive at last at the higher part of the East Rongbuk Glacier. God! This is exciting. We are making real progress. Our eyes are drawn miles up the glacier towards the fabled Kingdom of Ice. Every stretch of the way we are aware of the history involved with this route. Bruce, Mallory, Irvine, Finch, Shipton, Smythe, Somerville, Norton and scores of others, all followed this line. How spine-chilling to tread on the footsteps of these fine climbers. The only thing I don't fancy is coming across the tortured body of pour old Maurice Wilson.

There are giant ice fins, a hundred feet high on both sides of us and subsidiary glaciers reaching down towards us from a variety of peaks. At the base of each, in almost military formation, are blocks of frozen ice. This is a Magic Kingdom. The living glacier now twists and rises into a broken belt some two miles wide. As the mists

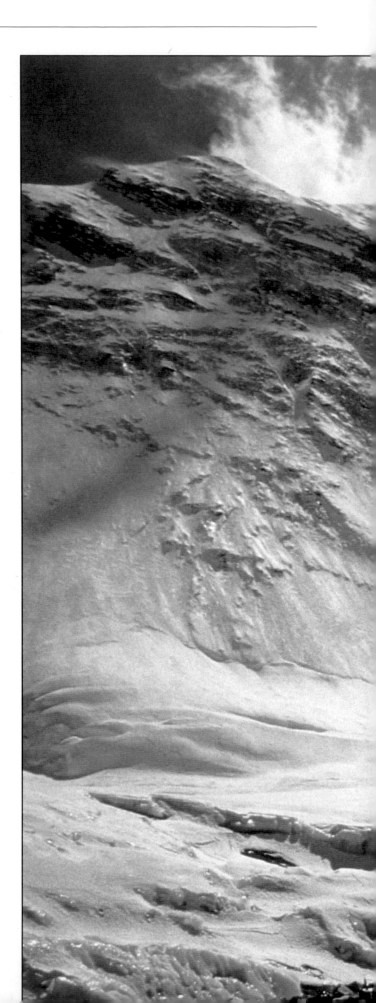

These pages: *Amidst high winds, yaks struggle over the broken terrain to arrive at our Camp III at 21,300 feet (6,390 m). Above them sprindrift snow blows across Everest's North East Ridge. The Pinnacles – one of the ridge's infamous features can be seen top centre.*

Left: *Oxygen cylinders stored and ready for use at Camp III. An ascent needs between 50 and 60 cylinders, depending on the policy of the expedition, and of course the number of climbers making the attempt. When full, these particular cylinders weigh 11 lbs (5 kg) each. The sets themselves only weigh 15 lbs (6 kg).*

clear, the giant shark fins of ice become more numerous. Fissures over 50 feet (15 m) deep appear. Crevasses – some narrow, some wide, bar our way and force us to make a detour. The route draws us seductively on, the scenery bewitches our eyes. Mountains on all sides! What monoliths of splendour surround us, their striking pristine form, releasing at their base huge energized glaciers; their ribbed blue flutings whisper far away songs in the gentle breeze and drops of ice delicately shower our bodies..

We are very close. Everest is cementing our friendship. On, on the winding path goes through the region of blue and green bergs and seracs. Can our senses take in more? We are at 20,000 feet (6,000 m) and moving in a dream. Look! Look! We marvel, as a single Lammergeyer flies overhead, showing the way to Chomolungma.

We are now moving into a landscape of glaring sun and ice. It is hard to understand but the brightest sunlight in England would be dusk by comparison. To take our goggles off in this region would, within minutes, result in serious sun blindness. Any exposed part of our bodies must be covered up and large quantities of cream applied to the face, neck, ears and nose. You even have to push cream up your nostrils otherwise the intense light will burn upwards toward your pituitary gland. Despite the need for protection, what a stunning, magical world the Fairy Kingdom of Ice is. We are entranced by fantastic shapes, as we move into the inner sanctum, which is rather like an Ice Palace. Here, ice pinnacles of iridescent green, blue, black, white and clear crystal soar around us.

Now we are in for a tough time. Steve has announced that we are about to enter the trough. I leave him to describe it: "The trough is a depression or natural snow and ice causeway, that runs for two miles up the continuation of the East Rongbuk Glacier. Imagine a corridor, 50 feet (15 m) deep and about 100 feet (30 m) wide, with steep sides of blue, green and white ice. At intervals there are lovely small glacial lakes that delight the eye. It is a remarkable feature and is the last obstacle to surmount before arriving at Camp III at 21,300 feet [6,390 m]."

The region is renowned for its stagnant, dead air and its fiery heat. It is now 1.00 p.m. The sky is clear and there is no cooling breeze. The stillness is almost frightening. Everest is situated at a low latitude of 28° North; the sun is now at its zenith and is beating down on us remorselessly. We enter the trough and the agony starts. Despite the liberal amounts of cream on our faces, we start cooking like roasting chickens and no amount of water can satisfy our thirst. Our throats become inflamed and painful. After half an hour we begin to stumble about like 90-year-olds, for there is no respite from the heat and the dreaded glacier lassitude forces us to move as if in slow motion. Even so, the scenery never ceases to inspire us and gradually and painfully we are getting there. Or are we? Climbing a hill of snow we find another to ascend, and another, and another, and . . . Another hundred yards and we sink into the deep snow, our hearts pumping madly. Then, as we crest the umpteenth hill, we see that we have done it!! We're out of the trough and there is the North Col.

Below: *Resting at 21,300 feet (6,390 m) and receiving instructions from the higher camps. Radio communication has proved invaluable to modern ascents. Five radios are usually taken on an average-sized expedition.*

To Camp III

The legendary North Col of Everest is before us. It looks so big. We sink into the snow and hug one another with emotion; it is a great feeling. Our speech is a little insane and feverish and in our excitement we forget that we still have half a mile to go to reach Camp III. But delighted to be out of the trough and pacing ourselves carefully, we do finally arrive at the Oh so welcome camp.

A large green mess tent has been erected and it is marvellous to hear the sounds of the high-altitude cook, assisted by some of the other Sherpas, preparing a meal. Later we enjoy the simple meal of noodles and omelettes, followed by litres of tea and coffee. No amount of liquid can satisfy our raging thirsts. Very little is said as we sit around on boulders, smiling contentedly, watching the flames of the cooker. Two hours later we retire to our tents, snuggle into our sleeping bags and fall soundly asleep. We wake periodically to the wind howling on the mighty North Col, only to doze off once more.

The following morning, I wake up to discover that I am sharing a tent with a cheerful Sherpa called Wongchu. I had obviously been so tired the night before that I had failed to notice his presence. He places a mug of sweet tea in my hands and I gratefully drink it down. I immediately want to urinate and am glad that I have my 'pee' bottle in my tent.

We are informed by Steve that today is a rest day for, after the efforts of the previous day, it is imperative that we allow our bodies to adjust to this extreme altitude. Food is already becoming unpalatable but we must eat, as we have each lost between 20-30 lbs (8-12 kg) in weight and we must maintain our strength. The only food I can tolerate is porridge, eggs and chocolate. Daniel Alessio, who is here at Camp III, informs us that at this height a distaste for meat is a symptom of disorder in the thyroid gland.

It is now important for us to move slowly and smoothly, as any quick action results in the body being

Below: *Preparing a meal at Camp III. Water is boiled using a pressurised gas heater for the preparation of dehydrated food or boil in the bag meals. One of the characteristics of cooking on expedition is that as altitude increases, so water boils at a lower temperature. In fact latter-day explorers would calculate their altitude by simply measuring the temperature of boiling water.*

Right: *Looking up to the North Col, with the North East Ridge above. The summit can be seen, top right.*

These pages: *The view up the North Face. The North East Ridge – our route – is on the left, while the Great Couloir is discernible in the centre with the Second Step visible above it on the skyline. The summit pyramid is to the right of the Step.*

convulsed by violent panting, followed by the heart beating like a hammer.

On to the North Col

By 8.00 a.m. the next day, we are dressed and ready to move off to the base of the North Col at about 21,500 feet (6,450 m). Our objective is to reach the Col itself at 23,150 feet (6,945 m), where Camp IV is situated. The Col looks vast and intimidating and it rises from the top of the East Rongbuk Glacier for about 2,000 feet (600 m). Near the top is a particularly tricky section that includes a rather daunting, long traverse, with a sheer drop of 1,000 feet (300 m). Still, there are ropes, which will prove a great help and reassurance.

This place is really dangerous and, as we set off, we can hear the occasional avalanche thundering down mighty Changtse's western flanks. It sounds like distant artillery. Unfortunately, we have had to say goodbye to two of our climbing party, who have developed bad colds and troublesome headaches. Steve has arranged for them to go down with Daniel Alessio and a Sherpa. I am informed that several of the Team are suffering from diarrhoea, which is debilitating at this height. However, they insist on pressing on and, for the time being, Steve and Barny have agreed to let them continue.

The wind has dropped and we make good progress up the upper reaches of the glacier. Now and again, we have to cross a delicate crevasse. Otherwise the going is easy. After an hour or so we reach the base of the North Col. "This is it," says Steve. "This is where the mountain starts in earnest." His words thrill us but at the same time make us very nervous. There is a marvellous feeling of occasion to it all.

This is the crunch – the acid test! We clip our Jumar to the fixed rope and attach our sling with a Karabiner on it for added protection. With our ice-axes at the ready we take our first step on to the Col. What a shock, though! It is extremely hard after the relative ease of ascending to the top of the glacier. We have been fooled into thinking that the rest of the climbing would be the same. It is steeper than we anticipated, with slopes of 70 degrees or more being commonplace. Our breathing is rapid and frightening. I am afraid that I am showing my age and I constantly slump in to the snow, shocked and frightened. My heart seems to be missing a beat and to be using every last ounce of its power to pump my blood, around my body. I'm not going to have a haemorrhage or heart attack, am I? Steve advises me to relax, not to panic, to go slower and to take shorter steps. "There is no rush Brian," he says with a smile. "We have got all day to get to the top."

His words reassure me and the frequent rests and shorter steps make a big difference. It is also helpful to know that we are all finding it tough. An hour or so passes and we are gradually getting higher. Steve tells us that we are at about 22,700 feet (6,810 m): "Keep your heads down, we are almost there."

The extremes of temperature are very irritating; one minute it is hot, then suddenly it is cold. We strip off garments one minute and the next have to put them back on again. This means that you also have to take your pack off and adjust the harness around your waist. I sometimes think that a mountaineer is nothing more than a beast of burden! "How are you feeling, Brian?" enquires Barney. "I'm fine, bloody fine. Nothing is going to stop me getting up the Col," I reply.

Brave words but we still have the exposed traverse and vertical finish to contend with!

Would you believe it! The traverse proves to be quite easy and madly enjoyable and one by one we ascend the 60-foot (18 m) vertical wall. Wouldn't Captain Noel be pleased? I think to myself. I have done quite well. God this is marvellous. Even if we don't get any higher – what an achievement to ascend the famed North Col.

My friends, you have all made such sacrifices and efforts to come on this expedition and you are now at Camp IV 23,150 feet (6,945 m) on Mount Everest. More importantly, we have got a whole afternoon and evening to relax and enjoy the views. We look down and up, left and right and our eyes glisten with excitement. There is the whole North Face of Everest, directly in front of us. It is the most awesome and stupendous sight. In this thin air we feel as though we can touch it. The silence and stillness is alive and holy.

Steve and Barny lead us quietly to our tents which are set in a snow hollow and for the rest of the afternoon we sit agog at the scenery and drink, drink, drink, until evening. Before turning in we marvel at the beautiful Himalayan night. Never have we seen the galaxy so devastatingly impressive. It is as if the stars are just a few yards above our heads. They shine so intensely that they seem to be emanating from some giant roman candle that is hidden behind Makalu. We must now try to rest and sleep. My tent companion, Wongchu, is having difficulty breathing and keeps making the most awful gurgling sounds, so he will have to descend in the morning. We can all expect to deteriorate appreciably now, for we are in the 'death zone'.

Moving into the 'Death Zone'

At 6.00 a.m. the next day we are once more on the move. Our destination is Camp V at 25,600 feet (7,680). We are

Right: *The track coming up from the left shows our route up along the North East Ridge. The First Step from here appears as a slight bump in the centre of the photograph, with the Second Step and the summit to the right. To give you an idea of the size of Everest, the black dots that appear along the track are people.*

still climbing without oxygen and this will be a tough day. We can't get out of our heads that we were very weak on the Col the day before. What chance now of going higher? Banish these thoughts; it is time to press on.

We move away from the Col and follow the line of fixed ropes. At first we descend a little way, then we ascend and arrive at the foot of the North Ridge. This is delightful. We are about to take our first steps on the North Ridge. Our hearts are beating steadily enough and our breathing is easy and smooth. There to our left, going on forever, is the staggering North East Ridge. We are taking small steps and slowly and effortlessly we gain height. Our luck continues with the weather, not a breath of wind or a cloud in the sky. It is a wonderful feeling to look across to our right and see the summit of the fabulous pyramid, shaped mountain, Pumori, which is 23,000 feet (6,900 m) high and is below us! We look down on the North Col. The tortuous moments of that ascent the day before are behind us.

On and on we ascend and after two hours, the sun shines gloriously on the whole North Face. What a spectacle of wonder it is! Ancient voices and sounds, far, far away seduce our minds with their haunting tones. We shake gently with happiness, as the reality of our situation penetrates our being. We are alive, awake, real, tangible. Our veins throb with blood. We are on the North Ridge of Everest! Higher and higher we go, feeling like ants, as we look up and across, unable to comprehend the sheer size of the massive structure we are climbing. It pulsates with energy. There is thankfully no ferocious wind, only awareness and stillness.

The going gets harder and we are surprised to find how steep certain sections are. It becomes even steeper and ferociously hard and we are up to our waists in deep snow. We stop to rest and take a long drink. The North Col is way below and the tents look like little dots. We are now at roughly the same height as the north peak of Changtse, directly across from us at about 24,780 feet (7,434 m). To our left, beyond Pumori and past the region of the West Rongbuk Glacier, is majestic Gyachung Kang at 25,990 feet (7,797 m), and further still, all white and dazzling Cho-Oyu at 26,880 feet (8,064 m). It is a titanic landscape on the roof of the world. On and on, this blue and white panorama stretches, silhouetted against the sky, as it follows the curvature of the earth.

We continue our ascent and an hour later we look down on Changtse's peak; we are at 25,000 feet (7,500 m). As we climb higher, we are free of the fixed ropes and unstable rock but it is hard to establish a rhythm, as rocky ledges force us to dodge and weave about. Our

supplies of water are exhausted and we are showing signs of dehydration. Then, with great relief, we see the red Hyperspace tents of Camp V. By the time we arrive the Sherpas, led by Nga Temba, have brewed the tea and we dump ourselves down, very tired but extremely satisfied. It is a relief, at this point, to know that we will soon be using the oxygen. We have all weakened somewhat over the last 200 feet, with some experiencing a feeling of suffocation, which in turn creates a feeling of panic and despair. Steve has noticed that two are gasping for breath and is worried about lungs and rib-cages. He has also detected that several members of the party are suffering

Previous pages: *As we climb ever higher, it is worth taking a few moments to look back. This is the view from the North Face, looking down onto the sweep of the North Col from where we have just come. The East Rongbuk Glacier is to the right, while Changste rises up from the North Col to the left.*

from depression and the insidious effects of hypoxia or oxygen starvation. George Mallory experienced similar symptoms in 1922:

> Our minds are not behaving as we would wish them to behave . . . it's an infernal mountain, cold and treacherous, quite frankly the game is not good enough . . . the risks of getting caught are too great . . . and the margin of strength when men are at such great heights is too small.

What you must keep in mind, my friends, is that we have made good progress and have what Mallory didn't have; modern tents, ropes, clothes, oxygen and knowledge of the route ahead. But it is steep and dangerous here and we must take care. The weather has taken a turn for the worse. Mist is rolling in at an alarming rate and it is time to 'batten down the hatches', for we are in for a terrible storm. With the sudden disappearance of the sun, it has become freezing cold. God! This is awful.

That's the idea, into our tents. Drink, drink, drink! Soup, tea, coffee and lemon juice. Focus your minds on preventing dehydration. Take your crampons off and leave them at the foot of your sleeping bag near the entrance to the tent. Remove your boots and warm the insides over the gas flame to dry out your perspiration and reduce the risk of frostbite. Now zip up the tent to keep the swirling snow out but don't do all this in a jerky manner. Try to move smoothly and calmly, all the while conserving energy, which we will achieve if we help one another.

It is imperative that we do so, and we can help each other prepare the oxygen for sleep. We must take it in turns to go outside to collect snow in a plastic bag, which will provide us with water. Melting the snow on the cooker is a long tedious business but I bet that you are all thankful for the 'pee' bottles now, eh? There is a toilet ten yards away, behind a rock but in this wind you must be careful about your aim or the consequences can be most uncomfortable! I am sorry to be so crude but we are not on a picnic. You all want to climb Everest and this is what it entails.

A Night in the Storm

Our immediate concern is the storm, which has become very fierce and is tearing at our bodies. If you feel the tent lifting at any point, then press your body against it; it could save you from plunging 8,000 feet (2,400 m) down the North Face. Sleep is impossible, so just try and rest.

After six hours, the wind at last begins to drop. I thought that it might be the end of the expedition, as you cannot stay at this height indefinitely. The oxygen is a great comfort. We have used about two litres during the night and it has been of great benefit and has warmed every part of our bodies. Without it we would have felt the intensity of the cold much more, despite our clothes and our sleeping bags.

By dawn the wind has finally dropped and Nga Temba, with whom I am now sharing a tent, prepares several brews, which I gratefully drink. I am indebted to him. What a wonderful race of people the Sherpas are.

Five hours later we are on the move again and head

Below: *On the Second Step, looking down towards the East Rongbuk Glacier on the left. Notice the track on the extreme right leading up the ridge.*

for the final camp at 27,300 feet (8,190 m). We now have the benefit of our Russian Poisk open-circuit oxygen apparatus, which weighs only 15 lbs (6 kg), but sadly the wind has risen again. That 'old wind, with the old anger' is not too bad but it hampers our progress over the mixed ground of snow, ice and rock. Thankfully, we are on fixed ropes, as the going is steep and the exposure intimidating. Despite our finest down clothing, the cold west wind that blows from Nepal across Tibet, penetrates to our bones and numbs our minds. The luxury of the scenery, that we had enjoyed the day before, has disappeared and we concentrate solely on each step . . . and survival. If the wind were to increase in velocity, we would have no option but to retire as quickly as possible down the mountain. We are praying that it doesn't, as we are doing so well. It would be cruel now if Everest were to hit us with all its might. So far, so good.

Checking Our Oxygen

Our route takes us upward for about 800 feet on the continuation of the North Ridge, close to the line that Mallory and Irvine took in 1924. We rest for a while and remove our oxygen masks so that we can have a lemon drink from our plastic bottles. The liquid inside is protected from freezing by a thin fleece jacket with a plastic outer skin. We also check our oxygen, as we have been climbing on two litres now for 2½ hours. This means that we have about four hours of oxygen left, just enough to get us to Camp VI, which is well stocked with oxygen for use on our summit attempt. It is comforting to have a Sherpa alongside keeping an eye on us every foot of the way and ready to supply a reserve bottle of oxygen should we need it. The marvellous organisational skills of Himalayan Kingdoms has payed off. Yet, we must not get over confident, as we are now high in the 'death zone' and anything can happen at any time. Steve and Barny check our oxygen apparatus regularly to make sure that the tube from the mask is not frozen up and impeding the flow of oxygen and, after our drink, they adjust our flow to three litres to assist with the increasing altitude. We move off once more.

We leave the North Ridge and traverse perilously right, underneath the North East Ridge. It is both exciting and frightening for, except for the odd small section, we are without fixed ropes. Nevertheless, each of us is roped to our respective Sherpa. It has started to snow and

Above and right: *Sealing yourself off from your surroundings with oxygen equipment can make the most talented mountaineer look more like a fighter pilot. It may make for safer climbing, but this denial of the mountain's natural conditions still rankles with some climbers, who would sooner cope with altitude by acclimatisation and tackle the mountain on its own terms.*

Left: *At 28,250 feet (8,475 m), at the base of the Second Step looking back down the ridge towards the First Step.*

visibility is not good. But it does have its compensations, for it prevents us from seeing the awesome steep North Face. This oxygen mask is not a pleasant thing to wear. I find that the moisture and spittle gathers inside mine and seeps out onto my beard to form long icicles. We are battling hard now, for the wind has increased in intensity and threatens to blow us down the slope. We must get out of it soon or we will be in danger of getting severe frostbite. I hope that you have put liberal amounts of sun-block on your nose and face. Several of you have leather nose protectors connected to your powerful sun glasses, which will be very helpful. Our woollen hats and fleece lined hoods will protect us from the deadly short-wave ultra-violet rays, which have a baneful effect on the body.

Steve and Barny are shouting: "Look, over there!" There perched on tiny terraced shelves are the red Quasar mountain tents of Camp VI. We've made it!

That evening we all experience the frightful discomfort of our 'eagle's nest' homes. I am quite a big lad, despite a weight loss of some 40 lbs (16 kg), and Nga Temba finds it difficult to manoeuvre around me in the small tent. I suppose you are all experiencing the same problem Our sense of excitement has disappeared, and has been replaced by a strange stillness that verges on depression. Not one of us can say that he or she feels well. We are all suffering in varying degrees from sinusitis, chronic sore throats, laryngitis and coughs. Aspirin compound with codeine is a useful treatment against severe headaches and diarrhoea, and cough lozenges give temporary relief to our throats. Hot tea and coffee cheer us up enormously and give us a feeling of hope as we realise that, even in our weakened state, we have a real chance of climbing to the summit.

If only the wind would drop! The temperature is below 30 degrees with a wind chill factor of 20, which is increasing steadily. Hour after hour passes. If this wind continues we must abandon the assault, for we cannot stay here for more than one day, and we only have sufficient oxygen for one summit attempt. If we succeed, we will retreat past this camp, down to Camp V and possibly to the North Col. If we run out of oxygen here at 27,300 feet (8,190 m) and fail to retreat within two days, then we will most certainly die. It is all or nothing my friends!

Steve, Barny and Nga Temba will decide in a few hours' time. The plan is to set off at 1.00 am. It is now 9.00 p.m. and time ticks slowly by. Each member of the team is deep, deep, deep in thought and prayer. Every half hour or so we remove our oxygen masks and pull back our balaclavas to listen. The wind is still there and howls derision at our feeble entreaties to 'go away'. Nga Temba looks at me with his harrowed, weather-worn face and shakes his head despondently. Time is running out. In spite of the cold I manage to nod off and dream of my family and friends back home.

I am suddenly bought back to reality. Nga Temba has the cooker blazing with life and a welcome hot drink is being pressed to my lips. "The wind has dropped, Barjee," he tells me, "we must get ready to go." All the Sherpas call me Barjee, it means 'Grandfather'! God! I feel so stiff and cold, I can't stop panting and shivering. My night oxygen has stopped and I fall about like a drunken man. Nga Temba is already dressed and painstakingly assists me to get ready.

We Attempt The Summit

After several brew ups and some porridge, I emerge, with mask in place and oxygen and headlight on, to join you for the final push for the summit. Adjusting our headlights, we follow Steve in a disciplined line and con-

tinue to traverse the North Face. Apart from the faint hiss of the oxygen and the crunch of our plastic boots in the soft newly fallen snow, all is quiet. We can see the new moon, with Venus sparkling alongside it. It is a thrilling sight and reinforces just what a great adventure we are on. Way above us I can see the endless rock and snow of the North East Ridge. I wonder if the people on the North Col below can see us? Our lights dance in the darkness, forming a winding trail toward the upper reaches of the mountain.

In about two hours, we reach a point 800 feet (240 m) below the First Step and commence the push upwards and slightly to the right towards the Ridge. There are 40 and 50 degree slopes here and the snow is quite deep and powdery. Steve signals for us to take it easy and to continue to exercise extreme caution as, although we are roped to our Sherpas, a slip here would be extremely difficult to arrest. Four hundred feet (120 m) more and we pause for a drink now. Wow! Slowly and surely we are getting there. Are we really going to get to the summit? Comparatively few people climb the mountain from Tibet.

Quite unexpectedly, we notice that we don't need our headlights any more and the sun's rays herald the most stunning dawn we have ever seen. The light in the sky fills our hearts with warmth. We feel humbled and rejuvenated.

To our right we can see Norton's Great Couloir and the Second Step, where Mallory and Irvine were last seen in 1924, and way beyond this, the final pyramid. In the thin air we feel that we can almost touch the Second Step. The sun's rays inspire us and, with a feeling of great optimism, we plough on with great determination. On, on, past the formidable Yellow Band and higher and higher toward the First Step. We traverse below this through exhausting snow conditions and finally, after a dangerous tricky ascent of about 400 feet (120 m), reach the base of the Second Step. Here, we pause once more and take in long gulps of lemon juice. Our hearts are in our mouths, because we have all longed to see the famous Second Step. The Step has a prow about 80 feet (24 m) high. We move closer and reach the aluminium ladder that was placed here by a Chinese-Tibetan Team, who successfully climbed the mountain in 1975. To the left of the ladder is a snow filled crack, which was climbed by a Chinese climber called Mr Xu, in 1960. It is felt that this is possibly the pitch that Mallory and Irvine used in 1924 but, of course, that is still open to debate.

Climbing The Second Step

One by one, we tentatively climb the firmly placed

Left: *The Chinese Ladder, roped to the mountain several yards from the Second Step, and making an effective breech in its defences. It will help us over one of the most technically difficult parts of our ascent.*

ladder and reach the rocks above. From here we ascend a small snow slope and stand on the top of the Second Step at 28,250 feet (8,550 m). We all feel very thrilled and very proud. A quick check of our oxygen reveals that we have two hours left and we slowly move upwards once again.

There is quite a breeze sweeping up from the Kangshung Face from our left but it is nothing serious. Though the summit is only 650 feet (195 m) away, we have at least double that distance to travel along the Ridge and summit pyramid. It is intensely cold and our oxygen masks keep filling up with ice, so we have to remove and clean them regularly. Doubts begin to fill our minds, as we realise just how much we still have to do. The summit looks so close in the thin air, yet every tortured step we take does not seem to get us any closer. We mustn't lose heart and should simply concentrate on placing one foot in front of the other. We will get there,

Above: *Dawn light on the East – or Kangshung – Face strikes the Second Step, and the summit pyramid to the right. It is about here – within sight of success – that Mallory and Irvine disappeared in 1924.*

Left: *From the Second Step a lone figure makes his way towards the summit pyramid, around a feature sometimes known as the Third Step. To stay well clear of the dangerous snow cornices overhanging the Kangshung Face to the left, the climber's route will take him on a traverse up the final snow slope to the rocky summit ridge to the right. Distances are deceptive here, because everything is foreshortened.*

Top right: *The final climb to the top of the summit pyramid itself. Great care is still needed, a tired climber can make a mistake, even at this stage.*

Bottom right: *A triumphant Steve Bell on the summit. We have made it at last.*

we must get there! Another 200 yards (180 m) and we change our oxygen bottles and then move on again, relentlessly. We 'turn' a rocky ice feature often referred to as the Third Step and move laboriously up the summit pyramid. It is alarmingly steep. Our backs, legs and arms are aching as we push on, taking it in turns to kick steps in the snow. No words are spoken, yet we all know, as if bonded together by one spirit, that we are going to make it.

My dear friends, we are breaking through the veil of the unknown to attain the dream of a lifetime. At times it is impossible to take more than one step without bending over double with the pain. Every step is a monumental effort of will. Try going on all fours. Yes! That's it, I'll carry on as I am, as I find it difficult to stand upright. What's that? Who is that madman waving his ice-axe in the wind? God it's Steve! He's on the summit.

To The Top of the World

A few more steps and the angle eases off for all of us. We have reached the highest point on earth. We sink down

Nothing above you in the whole world.

"This is the summit, crowning the day? How cool and quiet. We're not exultant; but delightful, joyful, soberly astonished . . . have we vanquished the enemy? None but ourselves. Have we won a Kingdom? No . . . and yes. We have achieved the ultimate satisfaction . . . fulfilled the destiny . . . to struggle and understand."

George Leigh Mallory

Spread out around us is that great 'ring of white fire', the Himalaya. Look north and we gaze down on great mountains and on across the barren lands of Tibet towards the horizon and the very curvature of the Earth.

Look south, and the Himalaya marches down into the foothill of Nepal. Dawn here throws great swathes of shadow across gigantic snow-covered peaks. Have you ever seen such a sight!

on the summit, which is only the size of a large billiard table, and cry and laugh like new born babies. We dry our tears and look about us.

"Om mani padme hum. Om mani padme hum," chant the Sherpas and we join them in their sacred chant. Now we look down on a 360° panoramic view of the Himalayas. What did the sage Nagasena say of it?

> Five thousand leagues around, with its ranges of eight and forty thousand peaks, the source of five hundred rivers, the dwelling place of the multitudes of mighty creatures, the producer of manifold perfumes, enriched with hundreds of magical drugs, the Himalayas are aloft, like a cloud, from the centre of the Earth.

We sit on the summit in silent contentment. With my back propped up against Nga Temba, I quietly murmur a few words by George Leigh Mallory:

> Is this the summit, crowning the day? How cool and quiet! We're not exultant; but delightful, joyful, soberly astonished . . . have we vanquished the enemy? None but ourselves . . . have we won a Kingdom? No . . . and yes. We have achieved the ultimate satisfaction . . . fulfilled the destiny . . . to struggle and to understand.

Five days later we are on a Nepalese aircraft, bound for London. Just five days after being on the summit of Everest! It hardly seems possible. For one of those days we discovered the reality of Kipling's saying that 'The wildest dreams of Kew are the facts of Kathmandu'. In fact we are still recovering from the celebrations. Our eyes gleam with joy and smiles of sheer bliss are on all our faces. Yet, do I detect a certain sadness? I know that you are all eager to see your loved ones but the prospect of once more entering that 'other' life doesn't thrill you at all. That fast life of TV, politics and loud, loud motorways looms closer by the minute. As you peer out of the window of the aeroplane, your eyes moisten with emotion, as you see the distant Himalayas. The image reminds you of what the astronauts once said when they viewed the scene from outer space: "The mountain complex of Central Asia illuminates the heart of the Continent like a circle of white fire."

Look! My fellow adventurers! I have borrowed the Nepalese captain from the flight deck of the plane. It's alright, the co-pilot has taken over. What instructions should I give him? I know! "Second star to the right and straight on till morning."

Right: *The descent and journey back to Nepal take place in a kind of dream. Days before we were on the roof of the world looking up at the stars, and then suddenly we're waiting for an aircraft to take us back to 'reality'. Never mind. We have had a great adventure, and with perseverance we'll be back one day. After all, the mountain will still be waiting . . .*

'This afternoon we go to see a gas drill. They have contrived a most wonderful apparatus which will make you die laughing. . . . I would gladly put a little money on Mallory to go to 25,000 feet without the assistance of four cylinders and a mask'.

ARTHUR HINKS DESCRIBES THE OXYGEN EQUIPMENT OF 1922[6]

EVEREST WITHOUT OXYGEN

In 1978, THE WORLD of exploration held its breath, for an Austrian Expedition, led by Wolfgang Nairz, was to attempt the well known South Col route. 'Well, what is so special about that', people asked. What made this enterprise unique was that attached to this expedition were two climbers who were going to attempt to climb Everest without the aid of artificial oxygen. The names of these two climbers were Reinhold Messner and Peter Habeler.

Reinhold Messner, born in 1944 in the South Tyrol, has rightly been acclaimed as the greatest living mountaineer, a description amply justified by his achievement in becoming the first man to ascend all fourteen of the world's 8,000 metre peaks, mountains over 26,000 feet in height, all without oxygen. He is also famed for the uncompromising way in which he seeks ever-fresh challenges and pushes back the frontiers of the possible. For him, these challenges have nothing to do with conquest but are about inner experiences and testing his abilities and strengths to the limit.

Messner personifies adventure more than anyone else alive today. Chris Bonington said to me that without doubt Messner was the greatest climber in the world and perhaps the greatest climber of all time.

Fearless innovators

Despite the confidence of both Messner and Habeler, the notion of attempting Everest without oxygen received

Above: *A Tibetan figure of bronze and semi-precious stones representing Padmasambhava (The Lotus Born). This Buddhist mystic is believed to have introduced Tantric Buddhism to Tibet from India, and to have founded the first Buddhist monastery there.*

Left: *Makalu and the Kangshung Valley seen from the Raphu La.*

Right: *Everest from the Kala Pattar peak (18,000 feet – 5,400 m). Facing us is the North West Ridge. The North Face is to the left, the South Face is on the right, and the South Col is on the right hand side.*

Facing page: Reinhold Messner at the Base Camp at K2. Between his ascent of Everest with Peter Habeler in 1978 and his solo climb in 1980, Messner successfully reached the summit of K2, one of the most difficult and dangerous of mountains, and the world's second highest. He completed a magnificent treble when he successfully climbed the third-highest mountain – Kanchenjunga – in 1982. He was the first man to achieve this feat.

no support from their friends. On the contrary, almost everybody, whether they were mountaineers, altitude physiologists or doctors, advised strongly against it. 'It just can't be done,' they said, 'the lack of oxygen at this altitude kills the brain cells after only a few minutes, and, what is more important, it destroys the cells needed for the most vital human functions. First of all your memory will be disturbed, then your speech centre, and finally you will lose your sight and hearing. Everest without oxygen is suicide.'

Experiments in decompression chambers had shown that at an altitude of about 26,000 feet (7,800 m) the capacity for controlled thinking and action disappears. Within a short time you become unconscious; on a mountain like Everest, death is certain. Many physiologists argue that through lack of oxygen, body cells as well as brain cells simply die off. Unlike body tissue which can regenerate itself, brain cells which have been destroyed are lost forever. British mountaineers who, before World War II had crossed the 26,000 feet (7,800 m) barrier without oxygen, came back with pronounced gaps in their memories.

On the positive side, Habeler and Messner received encouragement from Doctor 'Bull' Olz of the Austrian expedition, who was of the opinion that, although destroyed brain cells cannot regenerate, their function can be taken over by other brain cells. They drew strength too from the words of Sir Edmund Hillary who wrote in 1961, "Even the summit of Everest is not beyond the capacity of an unassisted man but the risks are enormous."

To add to the great oxygen controversy, Peter Lloyd, who was on the 1938 Everest expedition, said:

The reflection I find fascinating is that Everest is exactly the right height to provide the perfect physical challenge to the climber's strengths and endurance. Were it 1,000 feet [300 m] lower it would have been climbed in 1924. Were it 1,000 feet [300m] higher it would have been an engineering problem.

Well, despite the fact that the consensus of opinion judged the climb to be impossible, that 'perfect physical challenge' was met by Messner and Habeler during the spring of 1978. The story of the climb is splendidly told by both climbers in their books, *To The Top Of The World* by Messner and *Everest, Impossible Victory* by Habeler. From the titles of the books, you will gather that the two climbers confounded the doubters and reached the highest peak in the world without the use of oxygen. The climbing world raised their hats in salutation and rejoiced that the impossible had been achieved. These two wonderful young men walked that thin line between life and death and returned to tell the tale. Here is Messner's recollection of their first moments on the summit:

The flood of tears, after this enormous outflow of will-power, suddenly released everything. We lay side by side on the summit like two people who had both lost their heads at the same moment. Once more I was shaken with sobs. I could neither talk or think; however, I noticed how this deep spiritual emotion threw me into a new equilibrium. I am nothing more than a single narrow gasping lung, floating over the mists and the summits.

A meeting with Messner

As part of our BBC film *Galahad Of Everest* I met a number of mountaineering giants, including Bonington, Hunt, Captain Noel and Jim Whittaker, but my final and perhaps most treasured 'scalp' was Reinhold Messner himself. The Director, John Paul Davidson, thought that it would be a good idea to have Messner (The Master) advise me, Blessed (The Greenhorn) on how to climb Everest. As we neared his home, I felt shy and ridiculous and I was beginning to have second thoughts about the whole thing! The great man had just crossed the Antarctic on foot and would certainly be in no mood to talk to a novice like me. He would give me a few minutes on the telephone, he had said, no more.

This 'Siegfried of the Mountains' lived in a small castle near Medano, in the Italian Tyrol. We arrived early and the Director and his camera crew approached the impressive front door of the castle and attempted to make contact with the owner. There was no response; he was not at home. All the while, like the coward I am, I remained 200 yards (180 m) behind, hidden behind a boulder. After ten minutes a car arrived with a solitary figure inside. The door opened and Reinhold Messner emerged. His body was long and finely muscled and his long tousled brown hair flowed into a full light brown beard. The face, striking and noble, was a map of all his trails and adventures. His piercing eyes, set above high cheek bones, surveyed our alien car, and took in the camera crew, who stood transfixed. I presented myself to Herr Messner and said my prayers. Our eyes met and all was fine. Perhaps he recognized somebody who was as mad as he was himself. At all events, we got on famously.

"I am fortunate, Brian, to have these mountains so close . . . the high one there, I run up and down each day

for training. . . ." "You do what?" I gasped. It looked about 8,000 feet (2,400 m) and very steep. Later, with much pride and joy, I had a little scramble on the rocks with the great man. He treated me as an equal and not for a moment did he patronise me. Reinhold's English flows delightfully and he never loses the thread of what he is saying. It is as if his brain were a house with all the lights on. Alert, artistic, imaginative, philosophical and kind.

We had talked for so long that the sun was beginning to set and we were in danger of running out of film. I shall never forget his words:

When you are at the base of Everest, the last step is dependant on the first, and the first step is dependant on the last. It is a definite rule, we do not go up there to die. Oh no! Many people say we climb because we have a death wish. This is not true. Part of the reason that I climb is to extend the boundaries of the possible. True adventure also includes the possibility of failure. I feel that the

film that you are making is on the right lines. Following in the footsteps of Mallory, wearing the same clothes, is an acceptable adventure. I must confess that I have always been sceptical about documentation on film but you will find that when it is a matter of survival, you will forget the camera. Then it is no longer about success or failure – it is a question of life and death. Anyone who has not learned to distinguish between adventure and show, can go to the cinema instead of to Everest. You must understand, Brian, that we do not go to Everest to die, but to survive. Yes, we move on that thin edge of life and death but our objective is to get back safely. You are right to be frightened and to have nightmares, this is healthy and natural. I was frightened too, when I was going to Everest. This teaches you to show respect for the mountain. If you hallucinate, this is healthy also because if you are alone the brain is creating something tangible for you, to help to sustain you, so that you will not be alone. For instance, up

Above: *This is the terrain over which Messner was forced to traverse in 1980, and it is the view of the North Face you get if you are clinging on to its very front looking straight up. In this case the climber is a member of the 1984 Australian North Face Expedition manoeuvering himself towards the Great Couloir – seen left and right, above.*

Facing page: *The enormity of the upper section of the Great Couloir seen from the North Col.*

Right: *On 13 May, 1995, the first woman to climb Everest alone and without oxygen reached the mountain's summit. In a truly magnificent climb along the North Ridge route, British mountaineer 33-year-old Alison Hargreaves took three days to reach the summit from Advance Base Camp on the East Rongbuk Glacier. This was her second attempt at Everest. During autumn 1994 she had climbed the southern route but had had to turn back at 27,200 feet (8,500 m). Once she had climbed the summit, Hargreaves did not rest on her success. The following July she had arrived at Karakoram Base Camp and was preparing to climb K2. If all goes well she will attempt the third part of Messner's treble – Kangchenjunga – in 1996.*

there, my rucksack became my companion. It is a rule with me, that when I arrive at a mountain, if it smells bad, I turn back! I have learned to trust my instinct. If, for some reason, you suspect that something is wrong that day, obey that instinct and come down . . . there is always another day. On Everest, you must go slowly from the Tibetan plains, say 15,000 feet [4,500 m], to Base Camp at 17,000 feet [5,100 m]. There, you must stay ten days maybe. See how you feel, listen to your leader. In your case it is David Breashears, an excellent climber. From there, I recommend you to go to 19,500 feet [5,850 m], stay a night or two and come down to Base Camp again.

Throughout this, concentrate on your breathing. Watch me – see how I hyper-ventilate – you try it – good, good. After a further period of rest, try for Camp Three at 21,500 feet [6,450 m]. Then, after a nights rest, go for the North Col, 23,150 feet [6,945 m]. Afterwards, return all the way back to Base Camp again. Remember, if your breathing is right, then you will automatically strike the right rhythm in your walking and climbing. After a stay at Base Camp for eight days or so . . . go for it!

Messner's solo climb

And the great man's actions are as good as his words. Despite his magnificent climb with Habeler in 1978, Messner was convinced that the ultimate Everest ascent, solo and without oxygen, was achievable and that he was the man to do it.

In the spring of 1980, Messner travelled to Beijing to obtain permission to climb Everest's North Face. The French had already booked the Face during the autumn season, so Messner proposed he climb before them, *during* the monsoon. This was making a dangerous expedition even more hazardous, but nevertheless the Chinese – after payment of a suitably hefty fee – granted permission.

Messner's only companions on the expedition were to be his girlfriend Nena Holguin and a Chinese liaison officer. They were to assist him as far as Advance Base Camp at the foot of the North Col, but no higher. Messner intended to climb Everest without high camps or supply caches; his aim was to go to the top with only the equipment he could carry. The total weight in his racksack would be just 44 lbs (20 kg), and would include a tent, sleeping bag, mattress, stove and food, ice axe, crampons and camera.

Base Camp was set up at the end of June, but the monsoon snows were just too heavy to make any progress, and so Advance Base Camp was not established until 15 August. On 17 August Messner began his ascent. Despite falling into a crevasse on his way to the top of the North Col, that first day saw him climb 4,800 feet (1,500 m) onto the North Ridge.

On the second day he had planned to move onto the North East Ridge, but found the route to be impassable with snow. His only option was to attempt a traverse across the snow-laden North Face to the Great Couloir and then follow this up to the summit.

It was a journey of over a mile across a vast slope of snow which at any time could have swallowed him up in an avalanche. Thankfully he camped safely that evening at 26,900 feet (8,200 m). He had made the traverse, but he was worried that he had only climbed 1,280 feet (400 m). Despite his position, he would have to make his summit attempt the next day.

To make matters worse, the dawn saw a sharp deterioration in the volatile monsoon weather. Amongst dense cloud and under heavy snow he began to climb up the Great Couloir with nothing but his crampons, camera and ice axe. Everything else was left behind.

As he moved higher, so his sense of direction deserted him and he was left with just his physical will and psychological strength to keep him going. In a state of almost complete exhaustion, and climbing by then almost by instinct, he finally made the summit at 3 p.m. on the third day. The ultimate climb of Everest had been made.

Below: *Alison Hargreaves on her descent from the summit – which she achieved in one day. By coincidence, on her way down, at Camp III, she met Mallory's grandson who was attempting his own ascent. He made it to the top the very next day.*

Gearing Up For Everest

GENERAL CLOTHING REQUIREMENTS

Underwear – two sets of Long Johns and tee-shirts. Wool, cotton and silk are more comfortable than most synthetics

Salopettes/Trousers – Fibre pile or similar

Jacket – Fleece or fibre pile

Shell Clothing – One piece or jacket/salopette combination with hood, preferably Gortex. If one piece it must have plenty of ventilation zips

Down Balaclava – One light-weight in silk or synthetic fibre, one heavy-weight wool or fibre pile

Mitts – Two pairs wool or fibre pile

Down Mitts – Essential for warmth

Overmitts – Preferably heavy-duty Gortex large enough to fit over mitts, with snow-cuffs and wrist loops

Finger Gloves – At least 2 pairs, cotton or synthetic contact

Sun Hat – Peaked cap or wide brimmed hat

Scarf – For sun protection and snow proofing the neck. Silk or cotton

Socks – Three sets. A set is what you normally wear with your boots, ideally one thin pair and one thick, loop-stitch pair. A vapour barrier sock or plastic bag can be used between them to keep the thick socks dry

Boots – Plastic double boots, expedition type. Make sure they fit comfortably with socks and are roomy enough to take chemical footwarmers

Snow Gaiters – 'Yeti' gaiters ideal as they cover the whole boot. Ankle gaiters will also suffice

Neoprene Overboots – Essential insulation for the feet

Rain Jacket – Only required if your shell clothing does not include a water-proof jacket

Glacier Glasses/Snow Goggles – One pair with perhaps a spare lightweight pair in case of loss or damage

Sunglasses – Glacier glasses can double up for these

Face Mask – Thin neoprene skier's mask covering nose and face to protect from cold wind

OTHER GENERAL CLOTHING

Underwear
Socks
Shorts
Training shoes
Trousers
Shirts and tee-shirts
Trekking boots/shoes
Pullover
Handkerchiefs

CLIMBING EQUIPMENT

Crampons – One pair, clip on, 12 point, must fit boots reliably

Ice Axe – Strong and lightweight with wrist sling 50-60 cm

Harness – Lightweight sit harness

Jumar – One with a handle

Sling – One 25 mm tubular tape. With a 600 mm loop length

Karabiners – One screw gate, two snap links

Descendeur – Preferably these should be lightweight or stitch-plate

PERSONAL REPAIR KIT

Spare parts and adjusting tools to maintain your crampons

Sewing Kit – needles, nylon thread, canvas and rip stop patches

Miscellaneous – 10 meters of 2mm cord, several short straps

GENERAL EQUIPMENT

Daysack – For the trek and trekking peaks – capacity 30-40 litres

Rucksack – Suitable for light and heavy loads. Strong and comfortable with internal frame but not too heavy or complicated. Seventy litres minimum capacity

Sleeping Bag – Good quality down bag, preferably Gortex covered. A separate Gortex bivvy bag can be used for water-proofing and additional insulation

Sleeping Mat – Full length closed cell foam mat. In addition a 'thermorest' (with repair kit) is thoroughly recommended

Eating Gear – One litre capacity unbreakable plastic jug with wide base and handle. Two strong plastic spoons

Urine Bottle – Very essential! One litre, water tight with strong wide mouth. Plus small funnel for females

Water Bottle – One litre. Strong and water-tight

Thermos Flask – Preferably non-breakable

Penknife – Swiss Army knives are particularly useful

Ski Poles – One set, telescopic. Useful for walking on low-angle terrain. Strongly recommended

Head Torch – With two spare bulbs and batteries

Sun Screen – Two tubes, must be highest factor available. Preferably 25 but at least 15

Lip Block – Three sticks

Foot Powder – Important for keeping feet in good condition

Insect Repellant – One small bottle. Useful for leeches

Lighters – Two, for lighting stoves. Disposable

Stuff Sacks – Useful for storing clothing etc

Camera and Lenses – Protective bag essential. Bring spare batteries

Camera Film – Don't under-estimate your requirements; also remember lens tissues/brush

Toiletries – As required. Small mirror useful

Diary/Writing – Paper, pens, areogrammes, diary

Walkman and Tapes

Passport/Money/Travellers Cheques/Address Book

PERSONAL FIRST AID KIT

Painkillers – Paracetamol, Bruffen, aspirins

Vitamin A Cream – One tube, for split fingers

Cough Lozenges

Multi Vitamins – Enough for ten weeks

Wound Dressing – Several

Sticking Plasters – Assorted

Safety Pins – Large supply, various sizes

Gastrolite – Ten sachets – for dehydration. *Very important*

Antiseptic Cream – One small tube

Antibiotics – Two courses, one for chest and one for bowel infections

Aret/Lomotil – For diarrhoea

N.B. The Expedition Group Medical Kit will also contain more of the above, plus extensive supplies for a wide range of medical problems in cases of emergency.

DIET

Your diet is of some importance because there is always weight loss during a high altitude climb, and it is best to start the climb with just a little surplus body fat. Don't overdo the accumulation of this body fat, as you have to carry it up the mountain and feed it valuable oxygen! there is no definitive ideal pre-climb diet but it would be wise to eat strictly low-fat, high protein foods in the weeks before the climb. The main aid to acclimatisation is liquid – lots of it. Before departure, start drinking large quantities (of water!) to get used to forcing it down on the mountain.

Smoking is definitely prejudicial to acclimatisation.

THE EXPEDITION FOOD

This excludes specialist high-altitude food and local provisions.

50 kg Tinned Fish – salmon/sardines/mackerel fillets/tuna

50 kg Tinned Meat – corned beef/chopped ham/spicy meats

25 kg Salami/pepperoni sausage

10 kg smoked cheeses

20 kg Dehydrated fruit

20 kg Dehydrated mashed potato

40 kg Sauces/mustard/pickles/chutneys in jars and sachets

40 kg Baked beans

30 kg Tea bags/instant coffee/malted milk and chocolate drinks

20 kg Soups. All flavours – sachets, dehydrated

30 kg Bread mix – white/brown/wholemeal

30 kg Marmite/jam/marmalade/Bovril/honey/preserves

15 kg Cheese spreads in tubes

30 kg Boil in the bag meals. Assorted

40 kg Biscuits – 50 per cent savoury and 50 per cent sweet

25 kg Cakes

20 kg Butter/margarine spread

50 kg Chocolates and sweets. Assorted

20 kg Tinned bacon/ham

IMMUNISATION

At least six weeks before we depart you will need to consult your doctor to work out an immunisation schedule relevant to the Himalayas. You should normally be immunised against the following: Polio, Tetanus, Typhoid, Hepatitis A, Cholera, Malaria. Vaccinations against the following may be useful if your doctor thinks they are appropriate: Rabies, Meningitis, Japanese Encephalitis.

DENTAL CHECKS

It is most important that you have a thorough dental examination before the expedition and have any necessary treatment carried out. Dental treatment on the mountain is likely to be drastic and traumatic!

ALTITUDE

One any mountaineering expedition there is always a possibility of climbers contracting Acute Mountain Sickness (AMS). This is a condition in which the person may suffer from headaches, loss of appetite, lethargy, insomnia and nausea. This is actually caused by too rapid a gain in altitude. Although the expedition has been planned to avoid this, acclimatisation is very much a personal idiosyncrasy which is impossible to predict in any one person.

There is a drug that has been used in the prevention and treatment of AMS which is known to have positive and negative effects on personal acclimatisation. Unless climbers have used this drug with successful results in the past, we do not recommend that expedition members resort to it.

VISAS

There are two ways of obtaining a visa for Nepal. You can either obtain it in advance from the Nepal Embassy or buy a temporary visa on entry into Nepal. The fee for British Citizens is approximately ú15.00 and you will need to provide a passport size photograph. You should submit your passport, one photograph, a stamped addressed envelope and your visa fee. You will normally receive your visa within 3-4 weeks.

You will also need a Chinese visa, which can only be obtained after receipt of an official invitation from the Chinese Mountaineering Association. These invitations generally come through within two weeks of departure for the Expedition. The Chinese visa costs approximately ú35.00 for UK passport holders. Please also make sure that your passport is valid for the whole duration of your visit.

NON-BRITISH NATIONALS

The procedure for applying for a Nepalese visa may vary according to nationality, so please contact your own Nepal Embassy.

TREKKING PERMIT

It is useful to obtain this in advance and will save time at Kathmandu. Please complete the Trekking Permit form and return it, together with three passport size photographs and a photocopy of the last four pages (new style European) of your passport to your Trek Organiser.

AIR TRAVEL

Full details of your flight times will be sent to you one month before departure. Please arrive at the airport at least 2½ hours before take off time. Your expedition leaders will make themselves known to you at the check-in-area. They will have your flight tickets and handle the check-in for you. Your baggage allowance for both international and internal flights is 20kg. Any excess baggage charge will have to be borne by yourself.

MONEY

All aspects of the trip are covered in your inclusive cost. The amount of money you take with you depends on how much you intend to spend. Souvenir purchases aside, the sum of ú150/$300 should cover any extra costs. Main meals in Kathmandu, even at the very best restaurants, are inexpensive. You will not need any local money until you reach the hotel. Money should only be changed in licensed money changing establishments such as banks, hotels and airports. Travellers cheques generally have a slightly better rate than cash.

TIPPING

It is normal practice to leave a 10 per cent tip at restaurants and give a small tip of 2 to 5 rupees or equivalent to hotel staff for carrying your bags, opening doors etc. Do not tip taxi drivers.

SECURITY

Whilst the expedition organisers do what they can to ensure the security of baggage, it is ultimately up to each climber to ensure that their personal possessions are safe and secure throughout the expedition. Rucksacks should be tightly secured with their contents concealed from view. Do not attach items to the outside of your rucksack, as these are likely to disappear. Important items such as money, passports and other vital documents should be carried in a money belt or inside zip-pockets; particularly when touring cities and towns.

PHOTOGRAPHY

If you do not already possess a good quality camera, the

purchase of one is strongly recommended. The best combination is a robust SLR camera with a wide angle zoom lens and a telephoto zoom lens. You may also find it useful high up on the mountain, where the weight and bulk of an SLR camera could well be a hindrance, to use a pocket-sized camera with a good quality lens instead.

VISITOR IMPACT

When people from the West visit the Himalayas, particularly for the first time, they are best unaware, and at worst insensitive, to the environment, the local people, and their religions. We should be aware that in their eyes we are incomparably wealthy and that we have a strong effect on their way of thinking. Like it or not, they draw example from us, copy our habits and want what we have. It is therefore extremely important that, before visiting the Himalayas, we are aware of issues that will ultimately effect the preservation of the environment and it's peoples' culture.

1 Please do not litter the countryside. You will see the locals have no litter sense and it may be tempting to follow suit, but it is much better to set a good example. Elementary precautions should be that we burn our toilet paper.

2 It may be tempting to take for souvenirs things like interesting coloured rocks, mani stones (carved religious stones set in prayer walls), animal horns or antiques. Please leave the environment as you find it. Remember the maxim: "Leave nothing but footprints, kill nothing but time, shoot nothing but photographs".

3 Streams are, of course, the locals' water supply and we should avoid using detergent or polluting them in any way. When going to the toilet keep at least 20 metres away from the edge of the stream.

MEDICAL PREPARATIONS

Our expedition leaders carry comprehensive medical kits and some parties include a doctor or nurse. However, in the event of somebody becoming seriously ill or injured, the evacuation of the casualty could be difficult. We therefore discourage people who have serious medical problems from joining the expedition. If you are in any doubt about this, please consult your doctor.

INSURANCE COVER

It is necessary for all expedition members to take out adequate insurance cover. The premium for this is approximately £800 and can be arranged for you by your expedition organiser if you wish.

FLIGHTS

Although the expedition is scheduled to end on 2 June, we will try to arrange open ended flight tickets to give us more flexibility. If we are delayed on the mountain, we should not be stalled for any longer than one week. It would be ridiculous to deny ourselves the summit of Everest just for the sake of a few days and an airline ticket?

And now the big shock . . .
The cost to you for joining the expedition is $28,000 US dollars, or £18,500 pounds sterling

---

More information on fully serviced and guided expeditions and treks to the Himalayas and elsewhere can be obtained by contacting, for treks:

Himalayan Kingdoms Ltd.,
20 The Mall,
Clifton,
Bristol BS8 4DR,
United Kingdom

and for climbing expeditions:

Himalayan Kingdoms Expeditions,
Adjacent the Foundry,
45 Mowbray Street,
Sheffield S3 8EN,
United Kingdom

ACKNOWLEDGEMENTS

The publisher wishes to thank the following individuals, organisations and agencies for the use of photographs in this book. Photographs are credited by page number and position.

The following abbreviations have been used. Steve Bell: SB; Brian Blessed Collection: BB; John Cleare Mountain Camera: JCMC; Royal Geographical Society, London: RGS.

1: Werner Forman Archive, Philip Goldman Collection; **2**: JCMC; **3**: RGS; **5**: RGS; **6**: BB; **7**: SB; **8**, Top: Werner Forman Archive, Philip Goldman Collection, Left: Telegraph Colour Library; **9**: Telegraph Colour Library; **11**: RGS; **12**: BB; **13**, Top: Mary Evans Picture Library, Bottom: BB; **14**: RGS; **16, 17**: RGS; **18**, Top left and right: RGS, Bottom: BB; **19**, Left: RGS, Right: BB; **20**, Top: Werner Forman Archive, Bottom: BB; **21**: SB; **22, 23**, All: BB; **24**: BB; **25**, Top, Bottom right: BB, Bottom left: Popperfoto; **26**, Top: SB, Bottom: BB; **27**: SB; **28**, Top: Werner Forman Archive, Philip Goldman Collection, Bottom: BB; **29**: SB; **30, 31**, All: BB; **32**, Top: BB; **32-33**, Main Picture: SB; **34**: BB; **35**: SB; **36, 37**, All: SB; **38**: SB; **39**: SB; **40**: BB; **41**: SB; **42-43, 45**: SB; **46**: JCMC; **48, 49, 50, 51**: BB; **52**, Left: RGS, Right: SB; **53**, Left, Right: RGS, Centre: BB; **54**: RGS; **56, 58, 59, 61**: BB; **62**: RGS; **63, 64, 65**: BB; **66, 67**: RGS; **68, 69**: SB; **70**: RGS; **72, 73**: RGS; **74**: RGS; **75**: BB; **76-77, 78, 79**: SB; **80**, Top: RGS, Bottom: SB; **81**: Jon Tinker/OTT; **82**: BB; **83, 84, 85**: SB; **88**, Top: RGS, Bottom: SB; **89, 90, 91, 92, 93**, All: SB; **94, 95**, Bottom: Bruce Coleman; **95**, Top: SB; **96, 97**: SB; **99-109** inclusive: SB; **110**, Top: Bryan and Cherry Alexander Photography, Bottom: SB; **111**: Bryan and Cherry Alexander Photography; **112**, Top: BB; **112-113, 114-120**, inclusive: SB; **121, 122**: BB; **124-125**: SB; **126-127**: Jon Tinker/OTT; **128-129**: SB; **130-131**: Jon Tinker/OTT; **132, 133**: JCMC; **134-135, 136, 136-137**: Jon Tinker/OTT; **138. 139**. Top: Jon Tinker/OTT; **140-141**: SB; **142-143**: Jon Tinker/OTT; **144-145**: Jon Tinker/OTT; **146-147**: SB; **148**, Above: Werner Forman Archive, Philip Goldman Collection, Below: SB; **149, 150**: JCMC; **152, 153**: JCMC/Colin Monteath; **154, 155**: Press Association; **160**: RGS; Front and Back Endpapers: Telegraph Colour Library.

The publisher would particularly like to thank Jon Tinker for the use of the photographs of his approach to Everest's summit, taken during his ascent in 1993 as leader of an expedition organised by OTT Expeditions. More information on OTT mountaineering and trekking can be obtained from: OTT, 62 Nettleham Road, Sheffield S8 8SX, United Kingdom.

Notes: The chapter-opening quotations are taken from the following:
1. Dudley Green, *Mallory of Everest*, Faust Publishing Co., Ltd., 1990, page 89.
2. Walt Unsworth, *Everest*, The Oxford Illustrated Press, 1989, page 169.
3. John Hunt, *The Ascent of Everest*, Hodder & Stoughton, 1953, page 8.
4. Dudley Green, *Mallory of Everest*, page 91.
5. John Hunt, *The Ascent of Everest*, page 211.
6. Walt Unsworth, *Everest*, page 78.

Author's Acknowledgements
The writing of this book has proved to be an 'expedition' in its own right. A veritable voyage of discovery.

The pleasure I have derived from writing it has been in the memories it has evoked of people and events from Everest's astonishing history. My enjoyment has been made greater for the opportunity it has given me to renew my acquaintance with fellow lovers of adventure.

I am indebted to a huge number of people for their help, encouragement and advice in putting together this work. To name them I would need a book the size of Everest itself. Please forgive me for shirking this responsibility, forgive me also for not covering the entire history of the mountain – a mammoth task that is quite beyond me; for that great accomplishment I can do no better than recommend that you read Walt Unsworth's splendid book *Everest*.

My sole objective is to inspire you to find your own 'Everest'. I feel that the only danger in life is to not take the adventure.

P.S. I would like to sneak in a slow Tibetan bow to my Editor, Tony Hall, to Hildegard, and to Stephen my P.A.

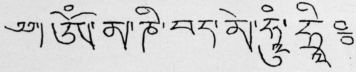

"Hail the jewel in the lotus"

Right: *Medal presented to the 1953 Everest expedition by the American Geographical Society of New York.*